A Captain's Daughter
The Memoir of a First-Generation American

by

Heljo Roos Vosari

DORRANCE PUBLISHING CO., INC.
PITTSBURGH, PENNSYLVANIA 15222

All Rights Reserved
Copyright © 2003 by Heljo Roos Vosari
No part of this book may be reproduced or transmitted
in any form or by any means, electronic or mechanical,
including photocopying, recording, or by any information
storage and retrieval system without permission in
writing from the publisher.

ISBN # 0-8059-6370-7
Printed in the United States of America

First Printing

For information or to order additional books, please write:
Dorrance Publishing Co., Inc.
701 Smithfield Street
Third Floor
Pittsburgh, Pennsylvania 15222-3906
U.S.A.
1-800-788-7654
Or visit our web site and on-line catalog at
www.dorrancepublishing.com

I dedicate this book to my parents, my husband, and the many wonderful people I have had the pleasure to meet on our Planet Earth.

Contents

Chapter 1: Once Upon a Time on a Small Island 1

Chapter 2: The Years in Shanghai 5

Chapter 3: Back in Estonia 15

Chapter 4: World War II and the Soviet Occupation 25

Chapter 5: The Nazi Occupation 38

Chapter 6: The Escape 47

Chapter 7: In the Old Kingdom of Sweden 53

Chapter 8: Starting All over in the USA .70

Map of Estonia 90

Chapter 1
Once Upon a Time on a Small Island

On the western coast of Estonia, a country in northern Europe, there are two larger islands and several smaller ones. My grandparents, Reedik and Emma Mänder, had a farm on the most western of these smaller islands, Vilsandi. It is about five miles long and two miles wide. It has a lighthouse and used to have about two dozen farms. A part of the island was covered by a forest.

Close to the lighthouse there was a sea rescue station. Many ships had run into the underwater rocks during stormy weather. When the alarm signal was sounded from the lighthouse, my grandfather, the captain of the rescue team, and all the other team members dropped everything that they had been doing and rushed to the rescue station. There they launched the large rescue boat and rowed it to the sinking ship to rescue as many seamen as possible. One of these, rescued from a Swedish ship, decided to marry my great-grandmother and stayed on the island.

My father, Siim Roos, was also an islander, born on one of the larger islands, Hiiumaa, as the fifth of nine children. Since the farms were not large, it was the custom that one son remained on the farm while the others found other occupations, often as seamen.

My father, like many others, continued his education in maritime schools both in Kuressaare and Riga, earning money during the required shipboard duty, some of which at the time had to be done on sailing ships, until he received his captain's diploma.

Estonia, at that time, was still under Russian rule and had no shipping fleet of its own except for coastal vessels. So his job search took him to Vladivostok in northeastern Russia, where he got a job with a German shipping company, sailing mostly between Vladivostok and various ports in China, Japan, and Indonesia.

My mother, Albertine, was born in Vilsandi. She was the youngest of eight children, four boys and four girls. Her oldest sister Hermine was an energetic and adventurous person. Wanting to see the world, at the age of sixteen she took a job on a sailing ship as a cook and eventually landed in New York City, where she met and married an Estonian who had arrived to the United States earlier. They settled down in New York City. When their first son was about a year old, Hermine decided to take a trip to Vilsandi to see her parents and show them their first grandchild. However, while she was enjoying her visit, World War I broke out and there was no easy way to return to the United States. The passenger ship traffic across the Atlantic Ocean was dangerous and no longer an option. The only possibility left was to travel across Russia to Vladivostok and to try to find a ship there that could take her to Alaska. From there it should have been relatively easy to make it back to Staten Island.

However this option, too, presented risks and difficulties. Russia was also in the war and in addition to that, there was the communist revolution going on, with warring "reds" and "whites" conquering cities and smaller communities, taking over trains and disrupting chances for normal travel. In addition Hermine, who had left home early, had never learned the Russian language. The Estonian language spoken at home was totally different, belonging to the Finno-Ugric group.

My mother, however, after completing her elementary schooling in the small schoolhouse in Vilsandi, was sent to a school in Riga where she learned to speak both German and Russian. So it was decided that she would have to accompany Hermine and her baby on the trip through Russia to Vladivostok and, if necessary, stay there until the end of the war. Vladivostok had a small Estonian community and two of her brothers who were also sea captains visited that port often with their ships.

Albertine was only sixteen at the time, but she must have felt that she had an important mission to do, helping her sister and the baby to get back to their home. So off they went and after a horrendous journey, including trains filled with soldiers and a derailment near Sverdlovsk, where many people were killed and injured, and many other adventures, they arrived safely to Vladivostok. Hermine and the baby managed to get to Alaska and continued by train all across the North American continent until they finally got to New York and back home.

My mother stayed on in Vladivostok, at first with her brother Peter's family and later with an Estonian couple who had no children of their own and who treated her very well. The couple owned a soap factory in Vladivostok and my mother started working in the office as a bookkeeper.

Then she met my father, Siim Roos. They fell in love and got married. Two years later my sister Aino was born.

Siim and Albertine Roos

In the Soviet Union, industries and private companies were nationalized, including the shipping company that my father was working for. He was still the captain, but the ship now belonged to "the people." Living and working conditions became more difficult and so my parents, as well as most other Estonians, decided to leave. When the ship was destined to leave for Shanghai, my father asked for permission to take his wife and daughter aboard so that he could take them to Shanghai. He was then given leave of absence and another captain was assigned to the ship. The family traveled to Shanghai and stayed there for a while.

However since the job situation there wasn't very promising either, it was decided that my pregnant mother and my sister would go back to Estonia and that if things did not improve, my father would follow later. This time they traveled by passenger ship. My father felt that it would be relatively easy for him to get a temporary job on a ship going to Europe.

Meanwhile World War I had ended.

When the revolution erupted in Russia in 1917, the Estonians, who had never lost their desire for freedom, decided to separate themselves from Russia and declared their independence on February 24, 1918. But it took them two more years of fighting, first against the Russians and then against the German Landeswehr, a special unit that was hoping to recapture the Baltic states. In 1920, finally the War of Independence was over and the newly formed Soviet Union recognized the independent Republic of Estonia "for all time."

Chapter 2
The Years in Shanghai

So it happened that I was born in the ancient town of Kuressaare, the capital of Saaremaa, the big island close to Vilsandi, on a Friday the thirteenth. The particular date, of course, did not mean anything to me until much later, when I began noticing remarks made by others.

"If you had only waited fifteen more minutes, it would have been Saturday the fourteenth," I was told later by my mother. I could not understand the difference, but there seemed to be something odd and unusual about the fact. I noticed later that my birthday occurred on a different day of the week every year and I remember wondering how could anyone remember what day of the week it had been. So I thought that my mother was probably just kidding.

Years later, when our math teacher demonstrated the "eternal calendar" and showed how to verify any specific date, I used the opportunity to do some checking of my own and came to the same conclusion. However by then I had heard that many people considered thirteen a lucky number and I felt that I should take it as a good omen—I suppose that I was always an optimist. And what else could I do!

I spent my earliest years on my grandparents' farm in Vilsandi, but I have only vague memories of that time. When I was three years old, my mother, my sister, and I embarked on a journey to the Far East. Shipping conditions had improved and my father had found a good job working for a Chinese company whose owner was said to be one of the richest men in Shanghai. So he arranged for us to join him in Shanghai. The trip took fifty-two days, first by passenger ship to Stettin in Germany, then by train from there to Marseilles in southern France, where we boarded a passenger ship that sailed through the Mediterranean, the Red Sea, and the Indian Ocean to Shanghai, making many port calls on the way. Unfortunately I was too young to remember much of that trip and to really enjoy it the way I would do it now. I do remember, however, that my fourth birthday was celebrated on the island of Sumatra and that I received an orange for a present. I also remember the tune "Valencia," which must have been a great hit at the time, for it was being constantly played by the ship's orchestra.

Shanghai, China's biggest port and a city of more than three million people, is situated on a tributary of the Yangtze River. It was at the time a very cosmopolitan city with about 50,000 foreigners living in various so-called concessions with their own administrations and schools in the northern part of the city. Many Chinese were living there, too. The southern parts of the city were predominantly Chinese.

The foreigners left in 1949, but I have heard that most of the buildings and parks of the former international area are still there and I was glad to read in the *New York Times* some time ago that the 1920s and 1930s are still regarded as "a most creative period in modern Chinese history" and the "height of Shanghai's glory."

We lived in the French concession on Route Vallon in a semi-detached four-story house. Another Estonian family, our distant cousins, were living there, too. They had two sons, Endel and Ivar, the same ages as Aino and I, so we had lots of company and could play interesting games together, some of which we invented ourselves.

Each house had a small fenced-off garden. There were about six or eight similar houses in the larger courtyard.

Our amah took care of the household, but my mother preferred to do the cooking herself.

Behind our house there was a high fence and behind the fence the property of a wealthy Chinese family. We children soon discovered that from the third floor window of the children's playroom we could take a peek into the beautiful gardens of our Chinese neighbor and see the shrines and the people walking there. This was our little secret.

Our school, the Collège Municipal Français de Shanghai, was within walking distance of our home and soon we were enrolled in the kindergarten. The school was operated according to the French system, starting with the grade twelve and working backwards to the first. Tests and homework were graded using a twenty-point system, with twenty being the best mark and zero the worst.

We had always spoken Estonian at home, but now French and English had to be learned quickly. Most of the studying was in the

Getting around in Shangai

French language, but every day there was also an English lesson, mostly reading and grammar.

It must have been difficult at first and I remember doing my homework in math and looking up words in the dictionary. My parents could not help me because they did not speak French.

However after a year in kindergarten and another in first grade, I must have done well enough in both English and French, because I spent only a month in the second grade and was then transferred to the third grade.

This is the grade that I remember best. My best friend was Yoshiko Grégoire. Her father was Belgian and her mother Japanese. We were both good students. When the director, Monsieur Grosbois, a veteran of the first world war, came into the class each month to distribute some kind of award cards, we always both received them.

The school population consisted of many nationalities, mostly European, but there were also Chinese students. The teachers were French, except for the British teachers who taught the English classes. At the end of the school year there was a ceremony, to which parents were also invited, for the distribution of prizes and books for each subject, if the final mark earned was a good one.

Then all the notebooks and paperwork were carried to the school yard for a big bonfire, which caused a lot of fun for all of us.

November 11 was a holiday, Armistice Day, celebrating the end of World War I. We all went to school with a bouquet of flowers, then marched two by two down Avenue Joffre and placed our bouquets on the tomb of the Unknown Soldier. It was a solemn occasion and it left a big impression on me.

In December we celebrated Christmas and we had a big Christmas tree in our living room. It was decorated by our parents and we were not allowed to see it before everything was completed. Only then the doors were opened and we could march in to admire it.

During those early years I was always the smallest and the youngest, but on Christmas Eve the order was reversed and so I was the first one to enter the living room. It seemed like such a great privilege to me! There were presents and paper hats and we all had great fun.

On February twenty-fourth we celebrated the Independence Day of Estonia, our home country. Often there were guests who joined us for the occasion.

Another important celebration was the Chinese New Year. In addition to street festivities, it was also a time for gift giving. Since my father had many Chinese business friends, he also received many gifts. I remember rickshaws driving to the door full of bolts of silk fabrics and ornaments, Chinese delicacies, and even live turkeys. The turkeys were running around in our little garden for a while until our amah took care of them and prepared them for dinner.

My father was also invited to other celebrations, such as the wedding of the daughter of the owner of his shipping company. I remember him talking about the large number of guests and the numerous dishes that were served and that it was necessary to try them all—to refuse would have been considered very rude.

Shanghai at the time had a population consisting of many nationalities. There were always people, probably friends or acquaintances of my parents, coming and going, sometimes staying with us in our top floor guest rooms for a short time until it was time to leave. We children did not know, of course, of the complicated political and economic conditions that may have been the cause for this. However occasionally we overheard some interesting stories which are still stuck in my memory. One of those involved two Estonians who were hiking through the Siberian wilderness, planning to cross the border into China. We listened with excitement to their description of the journey. They were camping outdoors one night, had just finished eating, and were ready to take a short nap when one of them threw a branch into the fire, which was almost dying. The flames flared up, there was a roar, and they saw a huge tiger, which had obviously been lurking nearby, leap into the darkness.

Summers in Shanghai were very hot and steamy. For that reason my parents preferred to spend some time during the summer vacation in Vladivostok, which they knew well and where they still had some Estonian friends who had decided to remain there. One of those families had a summer cottage, a so-called "dacha," not far from the city, which we could rent. Since my father usually had many scheduled trips with his ship between Shanghai and Vladivostok, getting there and back was no problem—we traveled with him. This also provided the opportunity to spend some more time with him since he was away from home a lot because of his occupation, usually for several weeks at a time.

When the ship arrived in Vladivostok, a large number of port authorities always came on board for customs clearance and other formalities. So my father asked the steward to have plenty of food available for the occasion and a lot of time was spent eating, drinking,

The Captain at work.

and engaging in "public relations." The steward had to set up a small table for my mother and us children, since there was no room for us at the large saloon table, where we usually had our meals on board. My parents also took a lot of food with them for ourselves and for their friends. Sometimes our cousins Endel and Ivar came along, too.

The cottage where we stayed was situated near a nice little beach. Every morning we walked downhill to the beach and spent hours there building sand castles and having fun in the shallow water. We sometimes caught tiny shrimp with our bathing caps, placed them in a small water hole carved in the sand, and watched them with curiosity before digging a canal that let them swim back to their "home."

There were many small buildings at the beach, obviously for changing clothes, but I don't remember ever seeing any other people. We were told that everybody was busy working. At the time the Soviet Union had a six-day work week, with every sixth day a free day. However, the sixth day was not the same for everybody and thus family members had no way of enjoying it together. We were also told that they often had to "volunteer" for some other work on their free day. Since we were too young to pay much attention to such things, most of it went in one ear and out the other, but I remember wondering by myself about this kind of a system.

One summer, when it was time to return to Shanghai, there was an unexpected change in the usual schedules for my father and instead of coming to Vladivostok, he had to go further north with his ship. Since there were no passenger ship connections between Vladivostok and Shanghai, arrangements were made for us to travel to Japan with a Swedish ship and to continue from there to Shanghai. Freighters always had an extra cabin or two for occasional passengers.

When we were about to embark on the Swedish steamer, while going through the usual formalities, my mother was asked whether she had any Russian money. She answered that she had 200 rubles. She was then told that it was forbidden to take rubles out of the country. Then one of the men belonging to the port authority who knew my father came to her and, with the wink of an eye, told her to just give him the money. This she did, as there was nothing else that she could do.

Later as we were sitting in our cabin on the Swedish steamer, my mother was very upset, almost close to tears. Here she was going on a trip with two children but no money. Credit cards and travelers checks did not exist at the time. How on earth was she going to continue the journey home to Shanghai?

When the ship had left the harbor and we were on the open sea there was a knock on the door. It was a stewardess. She said that a gentleman had given her an envelope and that she had been instructed to give it to my mother, but not before the ship was out of Vladivostok. The 200 rubles were inside the envelope and our troubles were solved for the time being. We had a good time on board the Swedish ship, played with the big German shepherd that the captain had acquired in some port, and made it without any problems to Kobe and Nagasaki. My parents had friends there, too, whom we visited briefly and I remember the crowded streets and the many shrines and temples. Then we boarded a passenger ship which would take us to Shanghai.

The departure from Japan was very dramatic and left an unforgettable impression. Streamers of different colors were thrown by passengers to their friends or relatives standing on the pier, and vice versa, holding on to one end of the paper ribbon or tying it to the railing of the ship. As the ship started pulling away from the pier, these streamers broke one by one. It was a lovely farewell.

We made it back to Shanghai in time for the new school year. Obviously the money was sufficient for the short trip.

Back in Vladivostok, however, the drama continued, as we heard later. An official of the port authority had gone to my father's friend and asked him what he had done with the money that my mother had given him. The man then walked to the cashier and said, winking an eye. "Will you please give me the 200 rubles that I gave you earlier today?"

The cashier had no idea what he was talking about, but luckily she did not ask any questions. These were extraordinary times and you had to think fast. She just took 200 rubles from the cash register and handed them over to the official. When my father got back to Vladivostok and heard of this, he of course reimbursed the people for the amount. This incident could have had serious consequences for everybody involved. Luckily there was still some trust among the Soviet people and they were willing to help each other.

We never had the feeling in Vladivostok that we were being watched. But later my father told how during one of the customs clearance sessions, he was asked by an official, jokingly, after a few drinks, "Do you want to know what your wife did while she was here in Vladivostok, where she went, and whom she talked to?"

That was certainly eye opening! After these incidents, we had no desire to go back to Vladivostok.

It was a different era with different customs and traditions. I remember a note that my mother found as she was going through some of my father's papers. The note was dated from an earlier period before the communist revolution and it was addressed to my father as captain of the ship. It asked him to come to the office upon his arrival to pick up the wages for the crew and to take with him three strong men, to carry it all. The wages at the time were paid out in silver coins. The note gave the total weight of the wages, but unfortunately I cannot remember it.

There was another interesting story about a cargo of gold, probably from Vladivostok to some other Far Eastern port, which my father once had to take care of. That time a number of fully armed soldiers were placed on board for protection against pirates. Things must have worked out all right, since I do not remember hearing of any further details.

I still have fond memories of Shanghai, however. Life went on and there was enough to do. It did seem to me, though, that the grown-ups had a rather dull life. We children at least had our games.

And I remember secretly wishing for a more interesting life, something more than the everyday "stuff."

Little did I know what was still ahead for me!

A View of Tallinn's "old town."

Chapter 3
Back in Estonia

Meanwhile our days in Shanghai were coming to an end. My father, my uncles, and some of their friends had decided to start their own shipping company and since Estonia was now an independent country, their dream and plan was to operate it under the blue, black, and white Estonian flag. It was decided that my father would be the one to get things rolling, so while the others stayed in the Far East for the time being, he resigned from his job and our family returned to Estonia. This time it was important to use the fastest and the least expensive way to do it—the Trans-Siberian Railroad.

In March 1930 we traveled with the *Hsin Ping An*, my father's ship, to Vladivostok, where we boarded the railroad car which was supposed to take us to Riga, Latvia. There was no direct railroad connection to Estonia.

We took several trunks and large suitcases with us and lots of food, mostly canned; also tea, sugar, and powdered milk, since at the time no food was available aboard the train.

The journey took eleven days. We spent time reading and looking out of the window of our compartment, but that became very boring after a while. Except for Lake Baikal, which was quite beautiful, the landscape was monotonous, mostly forests. To pass the time we started counting animals—horses, cows, dogs, etc.—that each of us children observed. By the time we reached the Latvian border, my count was around 110.

The railroad stations on the way were very crowded and we children did not leave the wagon after having jumped out at one station and landing waist-deep in snow.

Hot water was available at the stations and my father usually got us some for our tea. He tried to get something else too, but after a lot of hassles, managed to get only half a loaf of bread. So we were happy about the food that we had taken with us and made it last until the end of the journey.

Our railroad car did not take us to Riga after all. In Moscow we were told that we had to change over to another wagon. Surprisingly enough we got some help with our luggage, but only after my father made a big issue about the fact that we had been promised a direct car to Riga.

On the Latvian border we all had to get out and pass the border inspection. Then in Riga we boarded another train that took us to our destination, Tallinn, the capital of Estonia.

My sister and I spent the summer at the farm in Vilsandi, helping with the chores as much as we could. Although we had not forgotten our Estonian, we got some tutoring from the local school teacher in the Estonian grammar, which is quite complicated. In the fall, back in Tallinn, we enrolled in the Lycée Français, which our parents had chosen, so that we would not forget our French. Latin, German, and English were also taught in the school and the teaching was in Estonian, but starting with the fifth grade, French language and later French history and geography were taught by native French teachers.

We adjusted quickly to the new surroundings and to our new classmates. Our principal in Shanghai had given us very gracious letters of recommendation, so a new chapter in our lives was soon in full swing.

My parents had meanwhile rented an apartment in the city. My father was busy organizing the new company and soon he bought the first steamer and became its captain. Since the ship only rarely came to Tallinn, we spent our summer vacations on board the *SS Merisaar* sailing between various ports of the British isles and Scandinavia, Holland, and Belgium. This involved some travel by passenger ships and trains to the port, where the ship was loading or unloading and at the end of our vacation, traveling back to Tallinn from the closest port. Since the ship had its own schedule, we sometimes missed the first or the last day of school or even had to take an oral exam earlier than the rest of the class. The school officials went along with this because they understood our situation.

We enjoyed these summer months very much. My sister and I had a cabin for ourselves. We had a small radio, which was still a kind of novelty at the time, and there were books to read. I remember Tarzan stories, Wild West novels, "The Forsyte Saga," and books by Jack

London. It was also fun to spend time on the bridge, particularly when the ship was entering or leaving a port. And there was always time for sunbathing and for playing cards while at sea. So there was quite enough for us to do.

In the foreign ports there was always time for sightseeing and even for daytrips to London or some nearby resort. I was greatly impressed by the British Museum and Madame Tussaud's Wax Museum. And there was a seaside resort where we went swimming and where people sat in rows of chairs on the beach and were learning to sing "Stormy Weather." It seemed like a very strange song, but after hearing it many times everywhere, we ended up buying the record as a souvenir. We admired the castle in Edinburgh, the Tivoli Gardens in Copengagen, and the various towns in Finland and Sweden that we visited. Often there were beaches nearby where we could spend days swimming and relaxing. I even remember a terrible sunburn that I once got in Finland, north of the Arctic Circle.

The loading and unloading took usually two to three weeks since the cargo was mostly lumber and had to be carefully placed. This gave us lots of time to spend on land.

Then there was the excitement of learning where we would be going next. This we heard from our father after he had contacted the agents, who were involved with the scheduling of the ship.

Although the weather was usually good in summer, when we were on board there were also sometimes stormy days. We quickly learned that the best way to avoid seasickness was to eat normally, stay on the deck, and when feeling the slightest discomfort, to start singing or even humming to ourselves. I think that it had something to do with the hearing and the sense of balance, both located in the inner ear. Anyway it helped us to cope with the rolling and pitching of the ship.

On one occasion the storm lasted for three days. The cook could not prepare any food nor could it be served. The plates would not have stayed on the table, although there was a small railing around the edge of the dining table. We managed by eating sandwiches, cold cuts, and biscuits and found the whole experience rather enjoyable.

Sometimes we saw fishing boats in the North Sea. The men on the boats would signal by holding up fresh fish. The captain would signal back, slow down the speed of the ship, the fishing boat would come aside, and the bargaining would begin. The fishermen would show what kind of fish they had and an agreement would be reached—so much fish for two or three bottles of whiskey and several packs of cigarettes. Then a pail would be lowered to the boat with the payment and the pail was filled with fresh fish. I remember a halibut once which was about five feet long and a huge crab. These had to be hauled on board by winch and they were a wonderful addition to our regular menu.

The shipping company was doing quite well and more freighters were bought. My uncles and other relatives left Shanghai and returned to Estonia to participate in the operations, some as captains, others as part of the management.

Meanwhile my father's health was deteriorating. He experienced symptoms of heart trouble and he had the choice to become more involved in the management of the company and to stay on land, but he loved the sea and could not imagine sitting in an office all day. So he decided to stay on the ship for one more journey, this time to Portugal, and to see how he could cope with his illness.

Unfortunately, soon after leaving Lisbon, he had a fatal heart attack. The ship returned to Lisbon for official formalities, then sailed to Tallinn. We learned of the tragic news by telegram, but it took two more weeks until the ship arrived.

I was twelve years old at the time and those weeks, as well as the funeral that followed, were devastating. Although my father had been away a lot, we could still keep in touch by writing to him and he sent us letters and cards, often from very interesting places in far-away lands. He also got us interested in stamp collecting and geography was always one of my favorite subjects in school. The summers that we had spent aboard the *SS Merisaar* with him were full of wonderful experiences. He even taught us to type. He had a portable typewriter which he used for his correspondence and he showed us how to operate it using all ten fingers. We would then type up forms for him that he could fill in later and send to the home office, indicating the name of the ship, the time of the ship's arrival in a port, the type of cargo, the date of departure, etc. This was always done to confirm the telegrams, which were coded in order to save money.

My father was a person of authority and greatly respected by everybody on board. When he was angered by something that was done incorrectly, we were careful to stay out of his way. However he was a good father to us and even years later, when I started working myself, I occasionally met people who had known him and who, learning that I was his daughter, said some very nice things about him.

The thought that he was no longer there for us made me very sad. I also became worried—what would happen to us? How could we survive? Maybe my mother would have to go to work—but what could she do? As far as I knew then, she had always been a homemaker and it was hard to imagine what our life would be without my father.

Fortunately the situation was not quite as bad as I had thought. The shipping company, which by then had acquired several other ships, was doing quite well, and since my father had invested as much as possible in it, the dividends helped us to continue with our lives.

We spent many of the following summer vacations in Vilsandi. My grandparents were no longer alive and the farm was now managed by Aunt Alma, an older sister of my mother. At the time there were ten cows, three horses, five or six pigs, and around thirty sheep belonging to the farm. There was also a dog, a cat, and several chickens. We learned to milk the cows and each of us had a cow that was considered our responsibility. Mine was a black and white cow called Minnie. She became so used to me that I could sit down on the grass while milking her every morning and evening and she never budged. We were told later that when we left the farm at the end of summer, "our" cows at first refused to let the farm help milk them and would just walk away, sometimes upsetting the pail of milk.

During the summer, the cows and horses were set free to roam on the island and feed themselves, the pasture lands and forested areas being used by the whole village. Sometimes the cows walked home by themselves at milking time, but often we had to go looking for them. We walked through the woods to their favorite resting areas, listening for the sound of the bell tinkling around the neck of the oldest cow in order to get the right direction. There were, of course, also other cows from the other farms wandering around, so it was important to learn to recognize the sound of our own bell. There were days when it took us an hour or more before we located our herd, but usually we managed quite well. The group stayed together and went with us willingly.

Even more fun was to go looking for the horses when they were needed for farm work or for transportation, since there were no cars on the island. During their free time the horses liked to "hang out" with the other horses of the village. We took with us some slices of dark rye bread, which the horses loved. When we found the group, we called our horses by name, stretching out our hands with the bread. The horses would come and eat the bread, then we put on the bridles and lead them to a tree stump or a big rock so that we could then climb on their backs. It was great fun to ride back to the farm. However we were only allowed to ride two of the horses who were quite mild-mannered. The third horse, Dixie, was a very beautiful animal, dark colored with a white blaze on his face and white "socks," but he was young and more nervous and we were not permitted to even try to ride him. Having heard stories about his temperament, we felt it was better to obey, so when Dixie was needed at the farm, he would be led by the bridle alongside another horse. We really felt very important riding through the village.

When the work was done for the horses, they were just taken to the gate, the bridle was removed, and off they would gallop, neighing to find the other horses. Sometimes we could see the whole herd of about thirty or forty horses galloping by, manes flowing. It was a wonderful sight.

We helped to do some of the work—weeding the vegetable garden; picking the raspberries, gooseberries, and the red, white, and black currants; turning the hay so that it could dry, etc. Sometimes we went out very early in the morning to meet the fishermen who came back from their trips and helped to clean the nets.

But there was always time to go swimming in the afternoon. The southern shore of the island was within easy walking distance from the farm.

At the western end of the island, near the lighthouse, there were several tiny uninhabited isles which had become a bird sanctuary for seabirds. Different types of seagulls, arctic terns, and many other types of birds came in large numbers every spring to nest on these isles and scientists came from several European countries to study them. There were also lots of tourists. The lighthouse keeper, Captain Toom, and his assistants provided boat rides for the tourists to the Vaika Isles and a tour of the small museum that had been established near the lighthouse.

We visited the area too, usually when we had friends as houseguests, never tiring of watching the multitudes of seabirds and also examining the plants that were growing there. And since our family knew Captain Toom very well, we were always given a private tour of the Vaika Isles and of the museum, then treated with coffee and a special liqueur made of flowers that grew only on the isles. We also heard lots of stories of the birds and the scientists and saw the photographs that they had taken.

One of these stories in particular has stayed in my mind, namely that seagulls can count only up to number three. When a scientist who wanted to study the behavior of the seagulls was taken by boat to Vaika at nesting time, the seagulls watched the returning boat carefully and realized quickly enough that someone was still on the isle, even when a special hiding place had been built for the purpose of watching and photographing the birds without disturbing them. They would fly around screaming and remained very upset. But if four people went to the isle and three returned by boat, the birds seemed satisfied and did not worry about any trespasser.

During the summer the village people used to gather at a clearing in the woods on Saturday evenings for folk dancing to the tune of an accordion played by one of the villagers. We went a few times also, after having first learned the dances from the people on our own farm.

It was an idyllic lifestyle, where people helped each other and life seemed to go on as if it had always been that way and always would.

We also had the chance to take some trips with the freighters of the shipping company, like the one in 1936 to Finland, Belgium, and Holland and then to Archangel in the northern part of what was then the Soviet Union. The father of our cousins was the captain of that ship and his family was also on board.

In Finland we had the opportunity to try out the new motorboat that the ship had acquired. Together with the captain's children we rode out to small uninhabited islands of the Aland archipelago for swimming and sunbathing.

In Amsterdam we had a lot of fun touring the canals. Once the motor stopped and the boys had trouble getting it started again, meanwhile we were just drifting along, trying to keep out of the way of the barges and other canal traffic.

In Antwerp there was a huge outdoor pool where we often went swimming. There were also many interesting department stores for shopping.

The journey through the Norwegian fjord country was extremely beautiful and the long summer days and very short nights as we traveled north through the lovely scenery of mountains, fjords, and small villages made it very difficult to keep to any kind of normal schedules.

For that trip we were all registered as part of the crew—cook's aid, assistant to the stewardess, sailors, etc., because freighters were not supposed to be carrying passengers while in a Soviet port. Upon our arrival to Archangel, the ship had to wait at anchor outside of the actual port for "clearance." Around 2:00 A.M., a large motorboat full of port officials and other authorities arrived and they all came on board. We all had to get up and go out on the deck and together with the crew, we had to wait until one official who had gathered all the passports called us one by one, checking each person with the passport picture and then ordering the person to move to the other side. This procedure took several hours since the Soviets were not very familiar with the regular alphabet used in Europe and most other parts of the world. Meanwhile four or five other men searched the ship very thoroughly, even poking into coal bins with long steel rods. It was a very strange experience for us, since nothing like it had ever happened in any other port. We had to stand outside in the very cool night, tired and sleepy, almost shivering, until the search was completed. Only then were we allowed to go back to our cabins. I was told that they were looking for possible spies who could somehow be smuggled into the country. Of course they did not find anyone. The ship then proceeded to the pier and the loading could start. None of us were allowed to step on land, except for the captain, who had to report to port authorities.

The loading continued around the clock with three shifts and the job was therefore finished faster than in other ports. The workers seemed very tired and during a short break for a quick meal, some of them almost fell asleep. The captain, who could speak Russian, had a chance to talk to one of them and was told that the men had to work two eight-hour shifts, one after the other. When they left one ship and a tugboat came to pick them up with music blasting from loudspeakers, they did not go home, but to another ship for another eight-hour shift. In addition, although the Soviet Union officially had a six-day work week, with every sixth day a holiday, people in the work force had to volunteer for work on their day of rest and work in any other field where workers were needed. This resulted in teachers and office workers being sent to load freighters in the port or to some other work that they were not accustomed to and consequently, there were many accidents all the time.

On the ship's departure, the same procedure as on our arrival had to be completed, with passport control and search of the ship, this time probably for escapees. Again we stood waiting for hours, shivering in the polar night, which was not dark but still quite chilly. We were certainly glad when the anchor was raised and we could start the journey back to the civilized world.

During the summer of 1939 I had another chance to spend some months with my cousins' family on board the *SS Kuressaar*, sailing to

Drammen and Bodö in Norway and then to Murmansk in the Soviet Union, where the ship was scheduled to pick up a cargo of fertilizers destined to Poland. I remember hearing rumors that the Poles were really using it to make explosives, but that seemed rather far-fetched, at least to me.

We had a lovely time visiting Oslo and hiking in the hills surrounding Bodö, then, after passing the North Cape, we soon arrived in Murmansk. The same procedure had to be completed by the port authorities as previously in Archangel, again during the very early morning hours. But this time we were allowed one visit ashore together with the ship's captain.

Our curiosity was great, but we soon found out that there was nothing much to see or to do. The streets were unpaved and very dusty, the houses only small wooden buildings. The only store that I can remember was a food store with a window decoration of hams and sausages made of wood. It was all somewhat depressing and we were glad to get back to the ship, even more so when the loading was completed in only three days and we were ready to leave.

Back in the Polish port of Gdynia, we received mail from home and newspapers. There was talk of preparations for another war. The lights of Danzig were pointed out to us and there was something ominous about it. But it all seemed somehow unreal.

The sun was shining. The city, which at the time was Poland's only port, built after World War I, was new and had many lovely parks. There were preparations for an international motorcycle race and flags of the participating nations were being raised in one area. We discovered the Estonian flag among them, but to our surprise it was upside-down on the flagpole—with white on top (like in the Polish flag) instead of the blue. We were sure that this had to be the Estonian flag, since we did not know of any other flag with the same combination of blue, black, and white, and traveling on board ships you learn to recognize the flags of many nations.

So when we saw some workers in the park, we tried to explain the mistake to them. It was difficult at first, because they spoke only Polish. But one of us had a small Estonian flag pinned to the jacket and that helped. This cleared up the problem and the men quickly corrected the error.

Gdynia was full of tourists from other parts of Poland who came to see the new port and the atmosphere seemed quite light-hearted. There were caricatures of Adolf Hitler sold on the street. There was also a lot of amber—necklaces, bracelets, and pins—some with small insects visible inside. I bought several of these to take back to my family since that year my sister was on another trip and my mother was busy with other things.

After the unloading was completed, the ship was going back to Murmansk for another load on the same white powder, but I, as well as the captain and his family, left the ship in Lödingen in Northern Norway and continued by train to Helsinki. It was time to go back to school.

We stayed in Helsinki for a few days and the captain's family was monitoring the political situation. It seemed that things were getting serious. I did not get the whole picture, but they were discussing whether to go on to Tallinn or return to Norway and try to get back on the ship when it was returning from Murmansk. That worried me a lot, for I really wanted to go home.

Chapter 4
World War II and the Soviet Occupation

It was the end of August 1939. The clouds of war had thickened. Moscow gave ultimatums to Estonia, Latvia, and Lithuania about military bases on their territories. Without any hope of help from the outside world and trying to "save peace," the three small Baltic countries were forced to agree to these demands. For a while at least, things seemed to calm down and we all decided to return to Tallinn, only a four-hour ferry ride from Helsinki.

I went back to school. Life went on as usual at first, then the war broke out. We followed the action on the western front, listening to BBC a lot and trying not to worry too much about our own situation.

We were now living in our own home in Nõmme, a suburb of Tallinn, only about fifteen minutes from the city by bus or by train. Several years earlier, after moving a few times from one apartment to another in the city, my mother had decided to buy a lot in Nõmme and to have a house built according to our own needs and wishes. We took some part in the planning of the building and the landscaping of the garden. There were lots of pine trees, which were protected by law, but we could plant flowers around the large terrace and even build a pergola on one end of it. And there was a small patch for growing strawberries, which grew well in the sandy soil.

The first floor, where we lived, had an entrance hall, three bedrooms, a living room, a dining room, a bathroom, a powder room, a kitchen with a pantry, and a sun room, from which one could walk out to the terrace. The second floor had an almost similar design, except that instead of the sunroom there was a balcony and one of the bedrooms also had a small balcony. The second floor apartment was rented out.

During the winter we could often put on our cross-country skis at our gate and ski to the slopes. Usually there was enough snow. Since we had a shortened school day on Saturdays, Sundays were usually reserved for skiing. During the Christmas holidays, there was, of course, much more time to enjoy the winter sports.

In June 1940, after the end of the school year, I spent a few weeks with a girlfriend at a small summer resort in southern Estonia. We swam a lot, hiked on the trails, and had a good time.

But in Tallinn, meanwhile, a lot was happening. Demonstrations had been organized by the communist party, the government fell, and a new communist government was put in its place under threats and with the support of the Soviet army. The same thing happened in Latvia and Lithuania.

It was time for us to return home quickly and to await further developments of the situation. Everything seemed suddenly very uncertain and we had no idea of what was going to happen next. All of a sudden, we realized that we were now living in an occupied country. Our freedom had evaporated.

September, the start of my senior year in school, brought many changes. All private schools were eliminated. Our school was merged with another private school for boys and was renamed Tallinn's Seventh. The school was still in the same building and the classes were kept the same but our former principal was now our physics teacher and also our homeroom teacher, while the former music teacher became the new principal. Russian language and Constitution studies were now mandatory for all. There was a so-called "Red corner" on every floor of the building where communist slogans and similar propaganda was displayed.

Students tried to make fun of it. On the official Red Army Day there appeared a slogan in the Red corner: A RED HOT WELCOME TO THE RED ARMY. How or by whom it was placed there was never discovered. We all had a laugh out of it.

However the pranksters had to be extremely careful for the punishment was known to be harsh. One girl was expelled for trying to rearrange Stalin's moustache on a poster. And when workers started to dismantle a monument which commemorated students and teachers who had died in the War of Independence in 1918–1920, some students of a nearby school were arrested for throwing inkpots at the workers.

In the beginning of November we were ordered to participate in the parade celebrating the Russian revolution of 1917. The day was a holiday, but we had to come to our school anyway to get organized for the parade. Our homeroom teacher, knowing that there were no communists among us, talked with us very openly. He said that he understood how we felt about it, but that it was really not worth it to even try to stay home that day. Those who were absent needed a doctor's certificate to prove their inability to attend because of health problems. Otherwise they would be expelled from school.

So we all gathered together in the schoolyard for the march. The mood was somber. But we started to feel a little better about the situation when some clever guys found among the officially provided banners (the only ones allowed) two that seemed quite acceptable to us.

Instead of the usual proclamations glorifying the communist party, the Soviet Union, the Red Army, Father Stalin, Marx, and Engels, etc., one of the banners was LET US NEVER FORGET THE CAPITALIST ENVIRONMENT and the other LONG LIVE THE BRAVE YOUTH OF CHINA.

When we marched through the town with these banners, there were visible reactions from the people who had gathered to watch the parade. However, we felt that we had managed to beat the system somehow, if only a little.

The economic system was completely and very quickly changed. Banks and enterprises were nationalized, so were houses that exceeded a certain number of square meters of living space. Our house was just under that norm, so it remained in private ownership. Even so, we were told that we had too much space; only eight square meters per person (eighty-six square feet) were allowed, excluding hallways, kitchens, and bathrooms. Therefore two of the bedrooms had to be rented out. At least they did not divide up the rooms in Estonia, like the custom had been in the Soviet Union. My mother managed to rent one room to an art student from a smaller town in the south of Estonia who was a friend's friend. The other, however, went to a Russian woman, an engineer who was employed by the Red Army. Fortunately, she was away a lot at the army base, but it was still a rather uncomfortable situation to share our home like this with strangers. One of us girls had to sleep on the couch in the dining room, the other had to move in with my mother. We did this alternatively, week by week.

Our shipping company was, of course, also nationalized and all Estonian ships were ordered to go to the nearest Soviet port. One of our ships happened to be in Tallinn, another one in Murmansk. They were immediately taken over. A third one was attacked by the Germans, first by a submarine and when the torpedoes could not sink it, then the bombers were called to finish the job. This took place in the British channel. The crew, however, was saved and managed to get to a French port. One of the ships managed to stay in the free world in spite of threats against the captain and his family. It crossed the Atlantic several times and participated in convoys between United States and England.

Several of the executives of the shipping company were arrested, as well as many well-known people who had been active in politics or in the business world. These arrests always took place at night.

When the banks were nationalized, all savings accounts were frozen. During the first two months, a small amount of 200 kroons could be withdrawn and my mother had to stand in line for hours to get it. After that everything was confiscated and we had no other income than the small amount of rental money.

The winter of 1940–41 was unusually cold. The first snow fell in October, which was very early, and it did not completely melt until next spring. Since communist societies do not believe in any religion, Christmas was no longer a holiday. The Estonian people, mostly Protestants with a smaller segment of Eastern Orthodox and Roman Catholics, still celebrated the holidays quietly at home or participated in church services during evenings and weekends.

It was no longer permissible to "exploit" other people, so we could not use the services of a fellow who had previously helped us with snow shoveling. The houses that were still privately owned were specially watched by the militia, which had replaced the police, in order to ensure that the regulations were closely followed. We had a corner lot and to keep the sidewalks clean after a heavy snowfall, my sister and I had to get up at six o'clock in the morning and work for two hours shoveling the snow before going to school. My mother had a back problem and we felt that it was better for her not to get involved with snow shoveling. She had already enough to do with housekeeping and food shopping, which was becoming more difficult as many items started disappearing from the stores. Life in the occupied country was changing rapidly. Even the names of towns and streets had been changed. The Avenue of Freedom, where we lived, was now called the Avenue of the twenty-first of June, after the date of the communist take-over.

I graduated from high school *cum laude* in June 1941. During the pre-war years that would have guaranteed me entrance to a university without further entrance examinations. But now college was no longer an option, it was necessary to become a part of the "working people." This in itself did not bother me, because at the time I was not sure what I wanted to do in the future and the whole atmosphere was not the kind that would have encouraged any planning. I had always been interested in languages, but the prospect of becoming a teacher did not particularly thrill me and I did not see any other options in that field. I also had a great interest in astronomy, but I realized that possibilities of finding a job in that field were very limited in a small country like ours.

There was one dream that I had always had after reading books of discovery by famous explorers who had traveled through the jungles of Africa or the rain forests of South America or discovered hidden temples and civilizations in Central America or distant regions in Asia—that of becoming an explorer. My one fear had been that by the time that I was old enough to do it, there would be no so-called "white spots" left on the globe to explore. However this, too, had become an impossible dream.

So I felt that the best thing for me was to try to find a job. This, however, was far from easy. I went to several employment agencies. People there looked at my school records and immediately mentioned that the "Seventh" was a former private school. The next question was about my "social background." My father was no longer alive and I learned quickly not to give his occupation as a sea captain but simply mentioned that he was in the merchant marine. And my mother? She was a housewife and a homemaker, by Soviet terms a "parasite." So what did that make me look like?

After several weeks of disappointing job searches, I became very pessimistic about my prospects for the future. Then a former classmate called me and asked if I would like to have a job. She had gotten a job as a typist in a small factory that manufactured nails, chains, and barbed wire. It had previously been part of a larger consumer company, but was now a separate entity with its own office, and they needed an inventory bookkeeper. Meanwhile I had taken a short course in bookkeeping and was glad to apply for the job. There were no complicated formalities and I started working right away.

My sister, who had graduated earlier, had also gotten a job in an office and soon became engaged to a young man who was a manager in some other manufacturing company.

This first job of mine was rather unusual. The office occupied the top floor of the factory. At one end of the room there was a desk and a chair for the new director, a former worker, who did not seem to know much about the production or the planning and who was obviously placed in the leadership position for purely political reasons. Then there was the technical director, who took care of the production; an accounting manager, who was also my boss; my friend the typist; several other staff members and a messenger, altogether ten people. The messenger had to deliver the letters to the various government agencies and other recipients and pick up the mail for our factory, so he was out a lot. Whenever he came back to the office and the director happened to be away from his desk, either in the factory or attending some political meetings, we all gathered around the messenger to get the latest news of what he had heard or what was happening in the city. In many ways it was kind of exciting, because there were always things happening, things that were not directly related to the work, but rather to the political situation, which was constantly changing.

News of arrests became more numerous. Among those arrested was my sister's fiancé. Then one night there was a knock on the door. My mother had to open the door for the militia. The house had already been surrounded by armed sailors of the Soviet Navy. The man who had occupied one of our "extra" rooms after the student had returned to her home, was given two hours to get dressed and pack his things. We did not know anything about him, except that he was the acquaintance of a friend of ours. Apparently he had once been working for the government in the social services area. My mother had to be a witness for the arrest, which was very embarrassing to her and also to the elderly gentleman. There was nothing that she could do to help him. For a long time nobody knew what happened to him or any of the other victims. Only recently I learned that he had been shot together with many other government officials.

During the night of June fourteenth a massive deportation of tens of thousands of Estonians was implemented by the Soviets. These people were loaded into railroad cattle cars and deported to the vast regions of Siberia, men separated from women and children, to work in copper mines or other gulag enterprises, while the women and children ended up usually in colhoses, the collective state farms.

We all became very aware of the uncertainty and the danger of the situation. People became afraid to sleep at home and many friends and relatives came from the city, asking if they could spend the night in our house. My mother was a very kindhearted soul who never refused help to anyone in need and I remember one night when we had twenty-one "guests." Every sofa and chair was occupied and people did not care if they had to sleep on mattresses on the floor, as long as they were away from their own home. The communists rarely went looking for those who were not caught at home, at least during that summer. They simply did not have time for it.

The German forces had started their attack on Poland and the Soviet Union. They advanced very rapidly at first. Then when Poland, Lithuania, Latvia, and half of our small country were already occupied by the German Army, the front stabilized for a while. We had no idea what to expect, but were convinced that big changes were coming. People were hoping that since things were already so bad and could hardly get any worse, maybe it had to get better somehow.

What happened next was that the Soviets started to use civilians for fortification works to stop the German Army. We in our office were told to come to work on a following Monday prepared for a week of "field work" and to take with us a blanket and food for a week, although some food would be provided. The same thing happened in other work places. Since canned foods had disappeared from the stores long ago, there was very little food available for such a project, mostly bread, fresh cucumbers, and some cubes of sugar which we had saved.

On Monday morning we arrived to work in our ski suits and we were loaded on a bus—all of us except the director and the technical manager. We were not told where we were going, but we could see that the bus was moving in an easterly direction. After a few hours the bus stopped near a river. The job assigned to us was to fortify the riverbank.

We got spades and started to work, but not very efficiently since nobody knew what exactly we had to do. However, there were some armed Russian soldiers watching us, so we had to pretend at least that we were trying to do something.

The sound of cannon fire could be heard in the distance. At first it seemed to be far away, but in the afternoon it grew louder and seemed to come closer all the time. This made us very nervous. Although we had little chance to talk to each other, there was a possibility that if things got really serious, we could all be loaded on the bus and with no chance to protest, be taken to the Soviet Union. After all, Leningrad was not that far away.

Luckily this did not happen. In the late afternoon we were told to get into the bus, but it started driving westward, past Tallinn, to a small community called Harku, which was something like a nature reserve. We got some soup and tea and ate our bread, sharing what we had with each other. We stayed there overnight, sleeping in a barn. Although it was summer, the nights were quite chilly and I found it very uncomfortable.

The next day we spent most of the morning hours sitting on the grass and waiting for new orders. These arrived eventually and we were taken to a lovely little beach on the Gulf of Finland. We saw some big sand dunes and the men started working on these, while the women were told to bring branches from a forested area nearby. These branches were used for camouflage and we concluded that the Soviets were expecting a possible landing from the north, maybe from Finland. It seemed very unlikely to us that the Germans would be coming from that direction. We stayed in that area for the rest of the week. On Saturday the buses were supposed to pick us up and take us back to Tallinn so that we could spend the weekend at home.

However, the hours passed and there was no sign of any bus. We started worrying that maybe the buses would not come at all. All that we wanted was to get away from that place and to go home. We had already signed a paper that morning promising to come back on Monday morning. Talking things over with my girlfriend, the typist, we decided to walk home. We both lived in the same suburb west of the city and therefore closer to our temporary work site. We estimated that the distance could be about six to eight miles. In fact the tower for ski jumping, the location of which was well known to us, could be faintly seen above the treetops. Somehow we managed to convince the leader of the group that we did not live too far away and would prefer to walk home instead of waiting for the bus, which would still be taking us to the city. In addition we were secretly even more afraid that the bus might not come at all—then we would just have to stay there.

The weather that day was cool and windy and soon it started to rain. But once we were on our way, we felt much happier and we enjoyed our freedom. It was a long walk. We talked and we laughed a lot—it was great to feel like a normal human being again!

When we reached the ski-jumping area, my friend turned off on a road that took her to her home. I continued alone for another twenty minutes, then I was home, too.

My mother, who had heard nothing from me for a whole week, was very happy to see me. After a hot bath and a change of clothes, we sat down for a cup of tea. My mother told me of the political situation and the advancing frontline. In the evening my sister arrived. She, too, with others from her office, had been sent to another area for fortification work. Soon thereafter our cousins Endel and Ivar arrived from their job of setting up defenses against tanks. After everyone had had a hot bath, we talked a lot about our adventures, wondering what would be happening next. Nobody felt that the fortification work that we had been doing would really stop the German Army for very long.

After talking to their parents and hearing that everything was all right at home, our cousins left for the city. This was the usual procedure when someone had been away from home for a while, especially for men.

There were rumors that a group of civilian workers who had been working east of Tallinn, had been cut off by the advancing German forces. They had been loaded on buses and sent to Leningrad. That was the last thing that we wanted and I quickly made the decision not to go back to the work site on Monday, but to just stay at home and see what happened. Of course, I could not go to the office either, not even to pick up my monthly salary, of which I received only eighty percent anyway, since I was less than twenty years old. Risky as it was, this way I felt that I had at least some control over my life, and in the overall confusion I hoped that nobody would have the time to come looking for me.

My cousins, however, did go back to their work place for another week and so did my sister. Shortly thereafter a mobilization order was announced over the media for all men between seventeen and seventy. They had to report almost immediately for service in the Red Army.

We were very upset by this, thinking of our friends and our cousins. Who would want to fight for a communist government and a system that had already brought us such misery! It was like a death sentence! And yet it was extremely risky to disobey; that we knew.

We talked and we talked, but everything seemed pretty hopeless. Then my mother came up with a new idea. She felt that maybe it would be possible to build a little hide-away where the boys could stay for a short time—we could not imagine that the communist regime would be in power for very long.

It was certainly worth looking into that. But how to communicate it all to our cousins? The telephone was out of the question, for we knew that the calls could be monitored. I had to go to their home immediately. I only called to say that I was coming and to wait for me.

When I arrived at my cousins' apartment, I was met by a most depressing atmosphere. Their mother was crying and the boys were packing their backpacks. The mood was doom and gloom.

I asked my cousins if they were really planning to go and register for service in the Red Army. The answer was that there was no way out, nothing else that they could do. They knew that their family would be held responsible otherwise.

Then I unveiled my mother's plan. It was accepted almost immediately. The question now was how to get the boys to our house in Nõmme. We were sure that the roads were checked, as well as the trains and all the vehicles that were leaving the city. The bus was too risky and so was walking. So it was decided that maybe the best way would be to take the train and not from the central station, but from a smaller station that was fairly close to their home.

Thelma, their little sister, and I started walking toward that station. The boys followed at a short distance. We agreed that at the first sign of a checkpoint or any similar danger, Thelma would turn around and tell the boys to disappear. We would then have to find some other way. Luckily things went as planned, the train came soon, and we all got on the train.

There were two more stops for the train before the station that was closest to our home. At the second one of those stops two men of the militia came on board and started checking the ID papers of the riders. Luckily they started at the other end of the railroad car and people took a lot of time finding their papers, so things moved slowly. The men were only halfway through the car when the train stopped at our station and we quickly stepped out, breathing a sigh of relief. Again Thelma and I walked ahead and the boys followed, taking some short-cuts through some backyards and empty lots. It was important to get them into our house with as little attention as possible and without being noticed by neighbors or anyone else on the street—safer for them and also for us. We knew that we were dealing with a potentially dangerous situation which could affect us all.

My uncle, the father of the boys, had taken a bus from the city and arrived before us. He was already busy preparing the hide-away. It was lined with old rugs and blankets and the cousins spent the following nights in it. During the daytime they were inside the house but at the slightest sign of danger, they quickly returned to their hide-away. We practiced the procedure a few times until it was well drilled in and went very fast. Since the house was on a corner lot, we had good visibility for anyone approaching, at least during the daytime.

We were hoping that this situation would not continue for very long. With all the arrests, deportations, and all the other problems connected with the daily living, it was generally felt that there just had to be some kind of change soon.

How my mother managed to get food for us is still a mystery to me. It surely involved standing in line for hours whenever she heard that a nearby store had somehow managed to get a supply of some food product and also going to the market in the city to buy whatever happened to be available. There was a small bakery not far from us. They could only bake one ovenful of whole wheat bread a day, but if you were not there standing on line at the time when the breads went into the oven, there was no chance of getting anything. It was a constant hassle.

Our former strawberry patch was now growing potatoes and provided some basic nourishment. The rationing cards did not help much because most of the time the food items were not available in the stores. We were not starving, however, and the very limited menu did not bother us too much. We were much more concerned by the fact that the frontline did not seem to move. The northern half of our country was still ruled by the Soviet Union. In their desperation the communist government issued new orders all the time, which increased the confusion and the uncertainty. Almost daily we heard of some friends or acquaintances who had been arrested or deported, among them many of my former classmates and their families.

Then one day there was an order issued that everybody had to turn in their radios and take them to various designated places. This was a big shock for us, for we had relied on our radio to get news of the war and what was really happening in the world. Most of all we listened to BBC from England and also a French station called Radio Metropole. Now this possibility seemed to disappear, too. But it was too risky to disobey, so we packed our radio into the box with which it had come, wrote our name and address on the box, and carried it to a nearby schoolhouse. Now we no longer had any idea of what was going on. There were all kinds of rumors of course and no way of knowing whether they were true or not true.

One morning we started hearing artillery fire. It meant that the German Army was probably advancing from the south. A quarter of a mile north of us was the railroad track and, as we soon heard, the Soviets had an armored train moving back and forth on it and firing at the Germans. The Germans were firing back, trying to destroy the train. We were now in a crossfire and could clearly hear the actual sound of the firing, then the sound of the projectiles flying overhead, and soon thereafter the explosions. It was time to go down into our basement, which had been turned into a kind of shelter.

A house across the street from us was hit and started burning. There was no way of extinguishing the fire, but with the help of neighbors, the pines closest to the house were taken down in an effort to try to stop the fire from expanding to other houses. This succeeded and everybody went back to their shelters, meanwhile keeping a close watch over the developing situation.

This went on for a couple of days. Then everything quieted down and suddenly someone announced that there were German soldiers brushing their horses in the empty lot next to ours. People came out of their shelters and hiding places and we knew that one phase was over for us. No one really knew what the next phase would be like or what to expect.

While for us now in Nõmme one occupation had changed to another, Tallinn, the capital, was still held by the Soviet forces. There was intense fighting for another day or two, then the battle was over. The Soviet troops and the communist leaders were evacuated by the Red Navy, which pulled out of the harbor and took off toward Leningrad. But before they left, they blew up the central power plant in the capital. We heard the explosion. The next thing we knew was that we no longer had any electricity or any water. The water had been pumped by an electrically operated well situated near our property, supplying the area with running water. So these were our two most urgent problems now.

My sister and I quickly ran to the schoolhouse, where our radio had been deposited, found our box, and carried it home, glad about the fact that there had obviously not been enough time to take the radios out of the country. This had already happened in some areas. However without electricity our radio was useless for the time being.

One of our neighbors had an ordinary manually operated well on his property and he kindly supplied us with drinking water, which of course had to be carried back home. It took about a week to get the other well working again, probably with the help of a temporary generator. What a relief that was!

As far as electricity was concerned, that was a far greater problem. Civilians have a very low priority in an occupied country during a war. The candles were used up quickly. My mother managed to get a small oil lamp and some kerosene. We kept the lamp in the kitchen, where we sat in the evenings drinking tea and talking. And this was fall, so the darkest time of the year was still ahead!

Tallinn in August, 1941

Chapter 5
The Nazi Occupation

During the prewar days we had spent time in the evenings reading, knitting sweaters, or listening to the radio or the records. There were also movie houses showing American, French, and German movies. In addition there were theaters, the opera, and concerts to go to. Most well-known singers, pianists, and other musicians included Tallinn in their tours and student tickets were very inexpensive. So we had spent many evenings every month enjoying the various performances.

The war had brought changes to the cultural life. During the Soviet occupation there were only Russian movies available, which we did not want to see, and the opera house and the concert halls no longer had any foreign artists performing. But now there was very little left of all this.

As the days and weeks continued without electricity, I discovered to my surprise that I could play the piano for myself without needing any light or any notes, just improvising on some folk tunes and popular melodies, some of which I had heard on the BBC programs. Among those there was one favorite, particularly well suited for us.

"When the lights go on again, all over the world
And the ships will sail again, all over the world...."

I was very glad that I had learned enough from my years of piano lessons to be able to do this and really enjoyed it. Even my mother sometimes joined me in the darkness and asked me to play some of her favorite songs. With a little practice, it was not too difficult.

The lights did go on again, just before Christmas, and it was certainly the best gift for all of us after almost four months without electricity. I don't remember that there even were any other gifts. The stores were still empty and special coupons were only available to couples who got married and for newborn babies. The food situation continued to be very difficult. Most of the food that was produced in the country went to the German Army. Although we received rationing cards, such products as meat, butter, etc., were just not available most of the time. Even in restaurants the only "entrées" available without coupons were vegetables with fancy names, such as "turnip soufflé" or similar concoctions. And since my mother had all our rationing cards to be able to take advantage of any "lucky possibilities" to buy food, we did not have much choice at all.

The small manufacturing company where I had worked had been reunited with its former parent company and the office was eliminated. So my job had vanished and for a few months I was looking around for another. Then in December 1941, a friend of my father called and offered me a job with the shipping department of the Estonian Economy Directorium.

The country had very little shipping left, since most of it had been nationalized by the communist government and diverted to Soviet ports. Many had been sunk, including some of our former freighters. Still there were some smaller wooden coastal ships left and the former owners wanted them back, even the badly damaged ones. Also the ports and the lighthouses had to be put back into working order. Our shipping department took care of the formalities and handled correspondence with the local German authorities, getting the necessary permits, materials, etc. The staff consisted mainly of former Estonian navy officers, captains, and engineers who had lost their ships and some younger people who took care of the various clerical jobs. I was involved with many of these, including the translation of letters into German because a large part of business correspondence had to be in German, and while most people in the navies and merchant marines of the world speak English, they are usually not that familiar with the German language.

Soon I became the assistant to the staff member who was authorized to formally reprivatize all the remaining vessels to their former owners. It was an interesting job and I met several people who had known my father. I felt very much at home in that environment. There was a lot of camaraderie among the people working in the department.

We had a cafeteria at work where a simple lunch of family-style food was served, which in itself was a big plus. During the spring and summer many of us spent days during the weekend at the former summer place of somebody's family, planting and weeding vegetables for our cafeteria. There was a beach nearby for swimming and it was all rather informal and quite enjoyable.

Meanwhile there were some changes at home, too. The local German officials had discovered the files of the housing agency, where our two bedrooms were listed as "available." Those were immediately requisitioned by the German Army for officers who were on leave from the eastern front. We had nothing to say about it. Usually the temporary guests stayed for about a week. The officer got the larger room and his driver the smaller one. They ate their meals and spent their evenings in the city, so we did not see much of them. But even so, the atmosphere had become somewhat uneasy.

It was forbidden to listen to any allied radio stations. This was not strictly enforced, as far as we knew, and we still listened to the BBC and some other stations to get the news about the war. It was quite clear that the official German version did not give the whole picture of what was happening on the front or what was going on in the rest of the world.

I remember one time when the German officer who was staying in our house came home rather early while I was still listening to BBC. He immediately asked which station we were listening to. I answered that I was not sure, probably Switzerland, and kept turning the buttons from one station to another. To my great relief nothing more was said.

We followed the activities on the various frontlines very closely and as the months and the years went by, we became quite convinced but the German Army would be defeated. But while we had hoped for a victory by the Western allies, we had also somewhat naively hoped that this would restore the independence of our country. However, once the Germans started retreating, the Soviets showed every intention of reconquering their former empire. And who was there to stop them? In spite of declarations of freedom for all countries, these did not seem to include the three Baltic countries—Estonia, Latvia, and Lithuania.

The thought of another Soviet occupation was horrifying. And the daily struggle for food was getting worse.

Then one day an older brother of my father came to us with an unexpected proposal. He was hopeful he would be able to acquire a piglet from a farm. Although all the piglets had been requisitioned by the Germans at their birth, the farmer had been able to save one by telling the Germans that one piglet had died. My uncle suggested that we could try to raise the piglet in our basement for a few months in total secrecy, after which he would take care of the rest. The meat would be divided equally between his family and ours. This was a very risky enterprise, particularly since there were German officers living in our house. It may seem ridiculous now, but this kind of defiance could have meant the death sentence for everybody involved.

My mother decided to take the chance and agreed. A special area was fenced in for the piglet in our laundry room and it grew quite rapidly, eating grass and weeds and whatever else was available. We had a special code name for the piglet, calling it only Madame Rosa, even when speaking among us. Somehow we got away with it. The meat was salted and used very sparingly and it certainly improved the food supplies for a while. There was even a little to share with others.

As the German Army started its retreat, there was a new mobilization and Estonian units were formed, which took over the job of trying to hold the frontline. Former Estonian pilots had managed to get approval from the German authorities to form their own squadrons. New pilots, mechanics, and necessary personnel were trained to increase the size of the defending units. These units got supplies from the Germans but they were to be used solely for the defense of Estonia.

Early in 1944 my sister got married to a former co-worker and moved to the city. Five days later, on March 9, 1944, my mother and I got together with both of them to see a new movie about the life of Wolfgang Amadeus Mozart in one of Tallinn's centrally located movie houses. I had managed to get tickets through my work place and since most of the tickets were usually reserved for German authorities and army personnel, we were very glad to be able to see a good movie.

Half an hour after the start of the movie, it was interrupted by the sound of an air raid siren and we were told to go to a shelter. Instead of going to the shelter of the movie house, my sister and my brother-in-law suggested that we go to the shelter of their house, which was close by. There had been such air raid warnings before without much happening at all. We did not think that this was any more serious and we were just sorry about not being able to see the rest of the movie.

We then sat in the apartment for a while and when the sound of explosions and anti-aircraft fire became more intense, decided to go down to the shelter in the basement of the apartment house. There were others gathered there, too. I found a place to sit down next to a door that lead to another area in the basement.

We had not been there for very long before it became evident that bombs were falling and exploding all around us. I have no personal recollection of what happened next, but according to others in the shelter, one of the bombs fell so close to the house that the door next to me was blown off its hinges and knocked me down and out for a short time, along with some of the others. The electricity was cut off, too. Somehow we were helped up in the darkness and moved to another area in the shelter, which seemed to be in a better condition. I kept asking what happened and when it was explained to me, I still asked the same question over and over. The next thing that I do remember was my sister saying, "She doesn't understand anything anymore."

"What do you mean, I don't understand?" I protested.

And this time I did get the picture. I realized that I was all right, except for my left knee, which was hurting. I had sprained it badly during my last school year when our new gym teacher started us on a new program of acrobatics, which we were not used to, having previously spent the time in gym with rhythmic exercises, volley ball, and running. At the time nothing much could be done except cold compresses and bed rest, and it took several months before it was back to normal again. It must have been injured in the fall. But now there were other things to worry about. What was happening to our city and to our homes? This was no longer a minor air raid!

After a while, the bombing seemed to be over. Stepping out of the shelter, we saw that the sky was full of flares, which were still burning, the so-called "Stalin's lanterns," turning the night into an eerie kind of daylight. Of all the houses on one side of Harju street, one of the main thoroughfares of Tallinn, only two were still standing, including the one where our shelter had been, but even those two were so badly damaged, with large cracks in the walls, that they were no longer fit for living. The rest of the houses were in ruins. We wanted to get out of there fast!

My sister and brother-in-law stayed to find out what could be saved of their belongings, but my mother and I hurried to the central bus station to see if we could get home. We were told that the buses were not running. What about the trains? There was no way of knowing, so we hurried to the train station. We were told the same story—no trains were running and nobody knew when they would start running again. The taxis, of course, were impossible to find. So the only thing left for us was to start walking.

The city around us was burning. We saw people here and there who were trying to put out the flames with whatever means possible. We went through the "old town" section, which goes back to the fourteenth century, with its narrow streets paved with cobblestones. One of our old churches was burning. The steeple was gone and huge flames were shooting up toward the sky. All these fires created their own firestorm and the air was full of burning debris. I will never forget that sight! As we had to pass the area, we pulled our coats over our heads and ran as best we could.

Once we got further away from the central part of the city, things grew calmer, but there, too, whole sections of the city were burning. Later we learned that almost 500 people had been killed that night and more than 20,000 had lost their homes. The opera house and the wonderful concert hall were totally destroyed.

It took us more than an hour and a half to get to our own suburb. It was now past midnight. As we got closer, we saw that the house was still there, but it looked strange and different. The reason for this was that the large dining room window was broken and the thick blackout curtains were flapping in and out of the window.

Still, what a relief it was to be home again! I sank into a chair and felt that I could not walk another step. My knee was hurting badly and needed attention. The next thing was to do something about the broken window. I don't even remember what we did about it, probably fixed it up with some sheets of plywood.

Shortly after we had made it back home, there was another wave of Soviet bombers attacking our capital city. We watched with horror. Tallinn was not a military target, but a so-called open city, with about 100,000 inhabitants at the time. It is also historically a very interesting and rather unique city with its medieval towers and old walls and many churches. Luckily the "old town" had suffered relatively minor damage, as we later learned.

The following day my sister and her husband moved back to our home and we managed to get one bedroom back for our own use. Later that day, Nina, a former classmate and a very good friend of mine, came by with her mother. Their apartment house in the city had been totally destroyed during the air raid and the fire that followed and they had been able to save very little of their belongings. They stayed with us until they could find an apartment not far from us.

Life became more and more difficult. Soon the buses stopped running because there was no gasoline available for them anymore. To get to work in the city, we had to take the train and the trains were so full, that often people were standing on the steps outside. I remember riding to the city like that, hanging on to the railing with one hand and holding my hat with the other. In the evenings the trains sometimes sat in the station for hours and we had no way of knowing when they would start moving. Many times the only way to get back home was walking.

Then one day I got a bicycle from a colleague at work who knew somebody who had left the country. This was not the time to ask too many questions about such things. We had already heard that some people had illegally gone to Finland and to Sweden. Legally this was not possible, except for those who had some Swedish ancestry.

I had never had the chance or the need to learn to ride a bicycle. My mother did not think that they were safe and besides we were often away during the summer, either sailing with the ships or spending time on the farm in Vilsandi. So it took a few hours of training, before I felt comfortable riding it and could start using it for going to work.

My uncle Peter and his family had also managed to get to Sweden, early in 1944, probably with a boat from the island of Saaremaa. My uncle started to work on the assets of our former shipping company, some of which he believed could be recaptured in the free world. One day my mother got a letter from him through intermediaries asking for certain documents that he needed. There was no postal connection between Estonia and Sweden at the time. The letter was handed to me at work and the reply with the documents was to be returned as soon as possible. My mother found the necessary papers, wrote a letter to her brother, and I gave it to our intermediary, a former sea captain and a friend of the family.

A day or two later I was informed that the operator of the motorboat that was taking the reply back to Sweden had been caught by the Germans, all the letters had been confiscated, and I was told to go home immediately and warn my mother of possible consequences. I rushed home as fast as I could. I had barely spoken a few words to my mother about the incident when the doorbell rang. Outside was a Gestapo officer who asked for my mother and said that she had to go with him for a hearing. While he was waiting and my mother was getting ready in the bedroom, I managed to whisper some instructions to her, while at the same time talking loudly about other matters. They left and we had a very anxious afternoon and evening, not knowing when or if we would ever see her again. Shortly before midnight, to our great relief, my mother was back home again.

She had been asked about everything in the letter, which of course was written in Estonian, and about every person named in the letter by initial only. She was questioned not once, but several times by different people. My mother spoke German fluently and obviously she was able to convince the interrogators that the content of her letter was not political at all, but only concerned with a family business. So they finally let her go home.

Sometime during that summer, probably in the month of July, my mother asked us how we felt about leaving the country. She had been told by a family friend of a plan to escape to Sweden in a fishing boat. The boat would leave from Tallinn when the political situation became totally hopeless. It would be extremely risky and total secrecy was essential. Leaving from the islands could have been easier in some ways, but we had no way of getting there and no connections with people there who could arrange something like this.

But right from Tallinn? That was unheard of! At the same time, how could we refuse? The possibility of another Soviet occupation became more real every day and filled us with horror. Also, we were young and if my mother and obviously some others were willing to take the risk, then we certainly would go along with it, no matter what! There were no other options anyway.

Late in the summer, there were some transport and hospital ships leaving for Germany and sometimes they took civilians along, but we did not know on what conditions. And those ships were easy targets for Soviet airplanes. At least one of them was sunk by the Soviets, with a great loss of life.

To try to travel to Germany by land was rather hopeless too, for the route was already cut off by the Red Army. No other legal options existed. Earlier some men had escaped to Finland by boat or during the exceptionally cold winters of those years, by crossing the Bay of Finland on skis, whereafter many men joined the Finnish Army to continue the fight on their side. However that was no longer safe because the Finns and the Soviets were already negotiating for a peace treaty and Finland would certainly be pressured to return any Estonians. Besides, that was illegal too, just as going to Sweden was illegal, as far as Germans were concerned. The reasons for this were never clear to us. What difference did it make to the Germans? Did it show a lack of faith in the victory of the Third Reich? We did not know.

But if we had to make the decision to leave our home and start all over somewhere else, then we certainly found it preferable to do that in Sweden. Besides, it was a lot closer to Estonia. Most of us felt that the new Soviet occupation would not last or be allowed to last very long. Maybe in six months or so we could go back home! What optimists we were, in spite of everything!

The time for our escape was not clear either. It depended on the weather, which just then was much too good. The summer nights in northern Europe are quite short and not very dark at all—more like twilight—and any illegal activity would be easy to detect.

The waters of the Baltic sea were patrolled by the German Navy and by Soviet submarines. According to rumors, the Soviets would pick up any civilians they discovered, take them on board the submarine, and whisk them off to Leningrad. The Germans, however, would arrest the people, bring them back, and put them in prison. Both of these scenarios were very disturbing and unacceptable to us. So it was very important that things were done right. There would be no hope for a second chance.

I continued working as usual. One day as I was riding home on the bicycle, it got a flat tire. I got off the bike and started walking and pushing the bike along with me. Suddenly a young man who had passed me on his bike stopped and asked what was the matter. I told him and he offered to fix it. We sat down on the grassy slope and he took his kit and fixed the tire. It was awfully nice of him, since I could not have done it myself and did not even have the equipment to do it. We continued to ride together as he was living in the same suburb as I did, only a little further. As we came to my gate and stopped, he mentioned that it would be nice to get together again and introduced himself. His last name was Lill, which in Estonian means "flower." And my name in Estonian was "rose." We both laughed at the coincidence and I found it a little embarrassing. He had been such a gentleman and yet I could not mention that I might not be there for very long. So I gave him my phone number, knowing very well, that it was useless. It was really hard to keep quiet about our plans, but I had no choice.

Chapter 6
The Escape

On August 28, 1944, a colleague at work who was also a former sea captain told me that he would take me for a drive during the lunch hour. Once we were in the car, he said that a change in the weather was predicted and we would be leaving that night.

We drove to a place where I had never been before, as close as possible to the port where the fishing boats used to stay. We walked through some fields and came to a pier where some boats were fastened. The man pointed out one of them and unveiled the plan: A car would pick us up around midnight—my mother, my sister, and me; also my cousin Ellen and her two small sons—and drive us to the same spot where we had stopped. We should not get out together, since so many people walking around at night could attract attention. Therefore, I had to walk my cousin and her sons to the boat at first, then walk back alone through the fields and take another walk with my mother and my sister. We were allowed one small suitcase per person.

It is hard to describe the emotions that I felt. Finally something was happening! The wait was over. We were leaving. I did not want to think any further than that.

At home, we all were in a turmoil, though trying to keep cool. My mother called our cousin Ellen, telling her to come over to our house in the evening and to bring both of her sons with her. She knew what that meant. Her husband, a major in the Estonian Air Force, had been taken to the Soviet Union together with the other officers and his whereabouts were unknown.

What to put into that small suitcase? Some clothes, of course, and personal items, documents, and pictures. I took an album with pictures of friends and pulled some photos out of another bigger album, pictures of us all in Shanghai.

We had also been told that the trip was expected to take thirty-six hours and so we would need to take some food for that period. My mother packed what we had and my cousin baked some bread with her last supplies. At midnight we were ready. Everything went as planned.

The car arrived, picked us up, and took us to the place where I had been earlier that day. The sky was dark and cloudy while I took my walks through the fields, first with my cousin and the boys, then with my own family. As we arrived to the boat, somebody quickly helped us on board and then guided us down to the hold. There were no lights anywhere. In the darkness there were more people, all in complete silence. When we found some room for our suitcases, we placed them down and sat on the suitcases.

We waited in silence. Then, shortly before daybreak, there was some movement on the deck and the fishing boat sailed out of the port. After a few hours, when the land was out of sight, we were allowed to come up on the deck and stretch out, but only a few people at a time. Most of the passengers preferred not to do it.

There were thirty-six people on board—a crew of four, consisting of the sea captain mentioned earlier and three teenage boys—and then there were the thirty-two passengers of various ages, among them six young children. The youngest of the children was two years old and had been given sleeping pills to keep him quiet. I hardly knew any of the others.

The first day at sea started out quite well. The weather looked good enough, the sails were up, and we were sailing toward Sweden very nicely. The mood was upbeat among us all and we ate most of our provisions. The distance between Tallinn and Stockholm is about two hundred forty nautical miles and we were hoping to be there soon.

In the afternoon, however, the winds changed and started blowing from the west, increasing quickly to a terrible storm. There was thunder and lightning almost constantly. The motor of our boat was very weak, only four horsepower strong as I remember hearing, and in the afternoon we were told that it was impossible to make any headway at all. So the captain had to make the decision to turn around and look for a storm shelter. Otherwise we would be using up all our fuel and then start drifting on the Baltic Sea with no control at all.

This was terrible news! All our joy and happiness about a successful escape to freedom was greatly diminished. But what choice did we have? We ended up anchoring off shore from the Estonian island of Hiiumaa, sheltered by a peninsula that stretches north from the island. The waves were still strong enough to make some people seasick, but we escaped the wrath of the first storm of the fall season. We remained in that area for the next ten days. Every morning we tried to continue our journey. The anchor was heaved and the boat continued to the tip of the peninsula, but was always met with such strong winds that it was impossible to go on and we returned to our earlier anchoring spot. As the days progressed, with the same scenario day after day, the situation on board became more and more depressing.

The food supply was gone on the second day. The water supply was gone too, because the storm had destroyed the fresh water tank. We still had rainwater for drinking and on some evenings when I crept up to the deck, I remember drinking the rainwater that had gathered on top of some empty barrels which were placed there for camouflage. To alleviate our hunger, the crew tried to help out by using their own supplies. Twice they cooked a big pot of oatmeal with seawater. The Baltic Sea is not as salty as the big oceans, so this tasted delicious, but there was not enough of it since it had to be divided among the thirty-two passengers, and we only got about two spoonfuls each—maybe the children got a little more. Also twice during those days the crew served us boiled potatoes. Each of us got one potato and it was devoured with the skin.

Once we also got some coffee substitute made with seawater—no real coffee had been available for years. This concoction tasted pretty awful, but nobody complained. Under the circumstances, it was still better than nothing.

But even those supplies did not last very long. Nobody was prepared for this kind of emergency. One day some crew members rowed ashore with the dinghy to see if they could find some food. They returned with one loaf of rye bread, which was also divided up among us. And that was all the food that we had during those days. After a while even the feeling of hunger seemed to disappear.

What added to the misery was that there was no radio on board. No way of knowing what was happening on the mainland. The German patrol boats were still crisscrossing the area and every now and then, when one of them came close to us, we were told to keep absolutely quiet. Sound carries very well in water and any suspicious sound could have meant an end to our escapade.

There was not enough room to lie down properly, at least not all at the same time. Later my sister and I, who were in the fore of the boat where the "ceiling" was very low, found some room for stretching and sleeping among the ropes that were stored there.

There was very little talk among us. One day, when we returned from another attempt to continue our journey and the anchor was lowered again, my mother, who was usually not a pessimist, asked me, "Do you really believe that we'll ever get out of here?"

"Oh, of course!" I answered. "The storm can't last forever. We must just be patient a little longer!" I was trying to convince us both.

I was not afraid of the stormy weather, probably because we had over the years spent so much time on board ships. Much later I learned that this unusually strong and long-lasting storm had cost many lives—the exact number was of course unknown, but lots of debris from boats and dead bodies were later recovered by the people living on Gotland, a large Swedish island, and some other coastal areas.

But I was very much afraid that we might be discovered, either by Germans or by Soviets. We knew that there would be a terrible price to pay for our attempt to flee to freedom.

I lost count of the time; the days passed one after the other. Then one morning as the boat passed the tip of the peninsula, the wind had decreased somewhat, the sail was raised once again, and we were on our way! The next few hours were full of anxiety—was it really happening this time? Or would there be another disappointment waiting for us?

In the afternoon the sun came out for the first time in days and we were allowed to go on the deck—those who had the strength and the desire. We were now far enough in the international waters so that it was considered safe. It was indescribably wonderful to just sit on the deck and watch the boat gliding over the waves, which were still quite large but not as threatening as before.

Late in the afternoon a boat approached us—it was the Swedish Coast Guard. After a quick exchange of information between the Swedes and our captain, the Coast Guard took us in tow and we continued our trip westward. Now almost everybody was on the deck and there were happy faces all around. For the first time in almost two weeks we felt that we had made it to freedom! The future was still unclear, but at least the misery of the occupations was over.

Late in the evening we arrived at Svenska Högarna, a relatively small island with a lighthouse and the coast guard station. Our boat was going to stay there overnight and continue the next morning to the Swedish mainland. We were all invited for a cup of coffee at the coast guard station. Women with small children could stay there overnight, while the rest of us would have to sleep one more night on our boat—there simply was not enough room for all of us at the station.

We did not mind that at all! It was amazing how quickly the picture changed. We combed our hair, straightened our wrinkled clothes, and looked like any other group of people climbing over the rocky path toward the small house. The children had some problems—they took a few steps and landed on all fours several times. Obviously the days on the rolling boat had affected their sense of balance. It looked quite funny and we all laughed a lot. The rest of us, however, managed rather well.

We all sat down around a long table and had two delicious cups of coffee and two little sweet rolls each. It all tasted just wonderful. Of course we could have gladly eaten a dozen of these rolls, but nobody could really ask for a better welcome.

The next morning our boat was taken in tow again and after a few hours we arrived at a place on the mainland which had become a gathering and registration center for refugees. We stayed in Kummelnäs for three days. Then, while some of us who had already made other arrangements left on their own, most of us were sent to Holsbybrunn, a small resort area in southern Sweden where earlier in the century, people used to go during the summer to take the mineral waters of a spring. It was normally kept open in summer only and the season was over already. But that year the place was kept open during the whole winter as a camp for displaced people.

Towed by the Swedish Coast Guard

Our fishing boat safely arrived in Sweden.

Chapter 7
In the Old Kingdom of Sweden

There were several larger hotel-style buildings in Holsbybrunn and some small cottages, all of which were used to house the refugees. And many families with small children got a room in nearby private houses. There was also a central building with a large dining room and a kitchen.

My mother, my sister, and I got a room in one of the small cottages. Since it was really built for summer usage, there was only a fireplace for heating the cabin. During the winter we usually had to quickly get the fire going and jump back into bed until the place warmed up a little. But on the whole we were glad about the privacy and adjusted soon enough to our new surroundings.

There were about three hundred people in our camp, mostly Estonians, but also some Latvians and Lithuanians. Altogether about 25,000 Estonians escaped to Sweden during the fall of 1944, plus a somewhat smaller number of people from the two other Baltic countries, since most of the Latvian and Lithuanian refugees chose a shorter and easier land route to Germany.

The Swedes used every available lodging for the refugees and it is absolutely amazing how well they managed to do it, since nobody could have been prepared for this kind of "invasion." All of us who took part in it will always be extremely grateful to the "Old Kingdom," as it was usually called, and we will never forget it.

We were all assigned kitchen duty—setting the table, washing dishes, and similar jobs. During our free time we started to learn the Swedish language. One man who had some knowledge of it taught us the fundamentals of the pronunciation and the grammar and soon it was possible to start reading the newspaper and to understand what we were reading, at least the meaning if not every word. It was not very difficult, particularly if you already knew English and German and could find many similarities.

Every Saturday evening there was a coffee hour in the cafeteria. Since Estonians always love to sing and most have, at one time or another, been associated with some choral group, someone would often start singing and others would join in spontaneously, often in harmony.

Sometimes a few guys with a good sense of humor entertained us with songs about events that had happened in the camp during the week. And once four of us—my cousin, my sister, another friend, and I—got together and formed a group that we called "The Silly Sisters" and performed our own variation of a satirical song. We had a lot of fun preparing the lyrics and it was a big success.

The manager of the camp heard us singing and asked if we could learn some Swedish songs for the coming holidays. We agreed gladly. A choir was formed and we started learning the music and the words in Swedish.

The closest town to our camp was Vetlanda and on several occasions we took a trip to that small town. The distance was about five miles and a so-called rail bus made the journey several times a day. There was a movie house in the town and on one of these trips we discovered that an American movie was being presented, namely *Now Voyager* with Bette Davis. We had not seen an American movie in years and my sister and I wanted very much to see it. There was, however, a problem with that. The cinema had only one showing per evening, starting at eight o'clock and lasting about two hours. The last rail bus left Vetlanda at nine o'clock. There were no other buses and taxis we did not even think about. After discussing it over and over, we decided that we would walk back following the rails. My mother did not like the idea, but we both insisted that it would not be a problem.

So one evening we took the rail bus to Vetlanda and went to see the movie. We enjoyed it very much. When it was over, we went to the station where the rail bus arrived and departed and started walking on the railroad track. It was, of course, very dark, but the night was clear and starry. After what seemed like a long walk, we began to wonder whether we were really on the right track. We had seen a small station at about the halfway mark with no buildings or personnel, just an overhead roof and a bench where the rail bus made a stop only when requested. We thought, that we should have already covered that much distance, but nothing like that was in sight. What if we had mistakenly chosen a different track and were heading who knows where? There were woods on both sides and nobody to ask directions from.

It was a scary thought! Should we turn around and go back to the town? But that, too, seemed like a difficult choice. We decided to go ahead a little longer and if nothing like a station appeared in front of us, then we really would have to turn around. So we kept walking and finally came to the tiny station. We were very happy to see it, knowing that we had been going in the right direction. So we continued happily until suddenly we heard some very strange noises. What could that be? We had no idea and stopped cold, then continued very slowly and carefully until we arrived at a small clearing in the woods and saw a group of horses. The noises that we had heard came from the horses snorting—that's what it was! Well, we made it back to the camp without any other problems and felt quite satisfied with ourselves.

Certain foods like coffee, sugar, and bread, were rationed in Sweden at the time. We of course had no rationing cards, but we soon found out that there was a small bakery in Vetlanda where you could order a cake if you brought your own sugar. So we saved the sugar cubes provided for our morning coffee and ordered a cake for my birthday. It was the most beautiful cake that I have ever seen, covered with a layer of green marzipan and decorated with three pink roses placed over it, everything edible, even the stems and leaves. We had not tasted anything like it for years.

It had become a tradition to celebrate our birthdays together with the others who had been on our boat and shared our troubled getaway. As we were sitting after supper in our crowded little room and enjoying the cake, someone came by with big news. Earlier that day, a small plane with four young Estonians had landed on a farmer's field about five miles from our camp. The men had been taken to the police station in Vetlanda on their way to an internment camp for military personnel. Some people in our camp wanted to go and see if they could meet them and possibly find out some information about their family members or friends. The manager of our camp was willing to go and take along a few, even my sister, who knew one of the men, a good friend of her husband. I had no real reason to go, although I would have liked to see them and to hear more about their unusual story. However, the pilot of that plane was Helmut Vosari, my future husband, and he never let me forget my "lack of interest" for not coming by to take a look at him!

Although Sweden is a Protestant country, the feast of St. Lucia is celebrated everywhere on December 13, in homes, work places, and many communities. For us this was the first time to experience it and the small children in our camp were invited to participate in the entourage of Lucia, a young girl dressed in a long white gown with a crown of candles on her head. All the other lights were extinguished and as we started singing the "Santa Lucia" song, she entered the cafeteria, followed by little children also dressed in white and wearing hats decorated with silver stars, symbolizing the end of the darkest time of the year and the start of longer and brighter days ahead. It was a beautiful sight. Afterwards, according to the custom, coffee and specially baked little saffron breads were served.

On Christmas Eve there was a service led by a Swedish minister and our choir sang some well-known Christmas hymns and also the Swedish songs that we had learned. Our little performance was appreciated by the local residents, who had been invited to attend the event.

After supper, the people who had been on our boat gathered in our little cottage. Nobody wanted to be alone. We sat and talked and, of course, started to sing again, first Christmas songs, then other songs, one after the other, any song at all, that any one of us could think of and without repeating any that had already been sung that evening. This continued all night through. It was our first Christmas away from our homes and away from our country and nobody wanted to start thinking about previous holidays, friends and relatives whose fates and whereabouts were unknown, or about our own uncertain future. It was better to keep on singing and somehow there was always another song that one of us came up with and that almost everyone knew.

When finally daybreak arrived and people started leaving, many of the younger ones among us went out for a long walk. It was a most unusual Christmas and one that I shall never forget.

During that winter there was a fire in one of the apartment houses. We all ran out but did not know what to do to help. Then someone threw a snowball into the burning building and we all started to do the same, throwing snowballs right into the fire, since nothing else seemed to be available. It did look rather hopeless, considering the huge flames that we saw, but somehow it did help. By the time that the fire truck arrived from Vetlanda, the flames had almost disappeared and the firefighters could easily take care of the rest. Luckily nobody was hurt and the damage was relatively light. The Swedes appreciated our rather primitive but quick action.

Soon after the New Year we were told that the camp would be discontinued in spring and we would be on our own. Some representatives from nearby communities visited the camp to inform us about available work opportunities in manufacturing companies and soon smaller groups started leaving. My sister and her husband, who had only recently joined us, left the camp to go to Vetlanda, where my brother-in-law had gotten a job. When we heard of these departures into the unknown, our singing group accompanied them to the railbus station and sang the "Farewell Song," wishing them the best of luck. It was a little sad and we realized that we would probably never see most of them again.

Thinking that there would hardly be enough work for all of us in the small towns around us, my mother and I decided to go north to the Stockholm area, where we hoped to find more opportunities. There was, however, a housing shortage in Stockholm at the time and foreigners needed a permit to live there. So when we left the camp before Easter, we made a stop in Södertälje, a small town about twenty miles south of Stockholm where some of my former colleagues from the shipping department had already settled. With their help we found a room that we could rent from two older ladies.

The next thing was to look for work. I happened to see an ad in the newspaper for a clerical worker and though it required some nerve, I went for an interview. My Swedish was not perfect of course, but I felt that I could manage fairly well and had to take the chance.

The interview was with the local manager of a company that manufactured incandescent mantles. In Sweden these were used in lighthouses situated mostly on uninhabited islands on the Swedish coast and also by some railroads. But most of the production was exported all over the world—to Italy, Greece and other Mediterranean countries; Kuwait and Saudi Arabia; India, Hong Kong, Australia, South Africa, and several countries of South America. This made the knowledge of other languages very useful and, with some hesitation, or so it seemed to me, the manager decided to give it a try. He mentioned a salary which sounded fine to me and once again I had a job. It involved correspondence, orders, billing, and export formalities.

The company also had a small sales office in Stockholm where the director, Dr. Lindgren, and his staff handled most of the communication with foreign clients. Dr. Lindgren was fluent in many languages and some weeks after I had started working, he talked to me over the telephone and asked me about stenography. I replied that I had never learned stenography, but that I could certainly take a dictation, being used to quick notes with my own abbreviations. He then said that his secretary was ill and he would like to dictate a few letters over the telephone, then he would drive over later in the afternoon and sign them.

I had so far only heard about Dr. Lindgren but had never met him, so naturally I was a little nervous, yet I had to go ahead with the plan. So Dr. Lindgren dictated three letters, one in English, one in French, and the third one in German, telling me to get the full names and addresses of the clients from the files in our office.

Maybe it was also a test for me, but luckily everything went very well and by the time Dr. Lindgren, a tall, distinguished-looking man in his fifties, arrived, the letters were typed and ready for his signature. He seemed very satisfied and I was never paid the originally mentioned salary. Already the very first month the amount was rounded up to the next hundred and there were further raises every three months or so during the first year. Even later, I never had to ask for a raise. During the following years I was often asked to spend some weeks at a time in the Stockholm office of the firm when vacations or other reasons made it necessary. I enjoyed it for a change and received extra pay for transportation and lunch.

I got along very well with my Swedish colleagues. We had our coffee breaks in the afternoon and when one of us had a birthday or a namesday (which were celebrated in Sweden), that person had to bring some pastry or cake to go with the coffee. Since my name was not Swedish and not listed in the calendar, my colleagues decided to give me the Swedish name "Ingeborg," which was listed as the name for the day when I first started working at the firm. We had a lot of fun with it and I enjoyed my work in the company.

At the advice of my uncle Peter we filed applications for immigration to the United States of America. Although life in Sweden was pleasant enough, there was some uncertainty about it because of pressure from the Soviet Union to force the refugees from the occupied Baltic countries to return to their homelands. Soviet officials had visited the refugee camps and offered free trips back home. I don't know of anybody who was interested. Most people refused to meet with them and wanted nothing to do with them. The Swedish government had resisted all pressures so far, but we could not feel completely sure about the future.

My uncle, who had worked twenty-five years for Standard Oil in the Far East before retiring to Estonia, had escaped to Sweden earlier in 1944 with his family. They had filed their immigration papers immediately and two years later they sailed to the United States.

My aunt Hermine was already living in the USA and urged us to act quickly. They both sent all the affidavits that were needed for us. However we were told at the U.S. Embassy that they could not give us any quick answers. At the time the United States had a quota system and Estonia had a very small quota of only 114 people a year. Because of all the refugees in various displaced people camps in Germany and other European countries, the quota had already been used up until the year 2000. Life in Sweden was considered normal and therefore no special treatment could be expected. We were just put on a waiting list and once in a while we received some information from the embassy.

Later that summer I finally got acquainted with my future husband. He was also from Tallinn, had joined the Estonian Air Force unit, gotten a military pilot's training, and had spent most of the year 1944 flying military support missions from various small airports near the Eastern front. In October, when the situation became hopeless, their unit was ordered to relocate, first to Latvia, then to Lithuania, and finally to Heiligenbeil in East Prussia, as that part of Germany was then called. At that point they realized that they would no longer be able to defend their country against the invading Soviet forces. As far as Estonia and the other Baltic states were concerned, the war was over. They heard that their unit would be disbanded. Most of the airplanes were already emptied of fuel, which meant no more flying. Nobody was interested in fighting for Hitler's Germany and the mood was very low.

That's when some of them decided to try to make it to Sweden. Helmut, who had the reputation of being a very good pilot, was asked to join them and to be the pilot of the plane.

The planes were scattered in an area between bushes. Only two of them still had fuel in their tanks. None of the four had flown that type of airplane before. There was no runway, but there was no time to lose.

Early next morning they removed parachutes, weapons, and everything else removable from one of the planes in order to make room for all four and in spite of the thick fog which covered the area, the take-off succeeded. For a while there was a possibility that the Germans would try to shoot them down, but thanks to the fog, they soon felt safe and continued the flight toward Sweden. It was impossible to find an airport, since Sweden too was covered by the fog, and when their fuel was almost gone, the plane landed on a field not far from Holsbybrunn.

After spending some months in an internment camp, they were free to look for work. This is how, after some trials and errors, Helmut arrived in Södertälje, our little town, which was known to have some larger industries, among them Scania-Vabis (now Saab-Scania). He got a job in that company. Fate had to step in once more!

He was tall, strong, and handsome. We spent time together, taking long walks and becoming convinced that we were meant for each other.

Soon we became engaged and in the beginning of 1947, as soon as our apartment in a new building was ready for us, we got married, first in the town hall by the mayor and a few hours later in the old church by an Estonian minister. At the time the Estonian clergymen did not yet have the authority to perform legal marriages in Sweden, therefore a double ceremony became necessary. The wedding ceremony was simple enough, but walking down the aisle together to the tunes of Wagner and Mendelssohn was in itself a wonderfully uplifting experience to me. The music director, who usually played the organ at weddings, had asked me about the music and since those wedding marches were the only ones that we both knew, the decision was quick and easy. Later there was a small reception at home for friends and a few relatives. A new phase had started for both of us.

Helmut had gotten a new job in the engineering department of a big Swedish company and we both liked our jobs. During the weekends we took several bicycle trips in the surrounding countryside and soon Helmut discovered a flying club in our own town where the members built gliders during the winter season and flew them during the summer at a small airport about an hour's drive from Södertälje. Courses were arranged for beginners and those who already had their "wings" were provided with opportunities to enjoy their hobby. Helmut, who loved the sport and had been actively involved with it already in Estonia, became a member of the club and we spent many Sundays at the airport. In addition to soaring, he soon acquired the necessary license for towing the sail planes to the desired altitude. He loved all those activities and even talked me into taking a course in flying gliders.

Our club did not have any two-seated gliders at the time. Therefore all the theoretical instructions had to be given first on the ground. Then you were towed by a jeep, sitting in a "fool-proof" trainer to get the feel of it, after which you were supposed to use the

Our wedding.

Last instructions before take-off in the trainer.

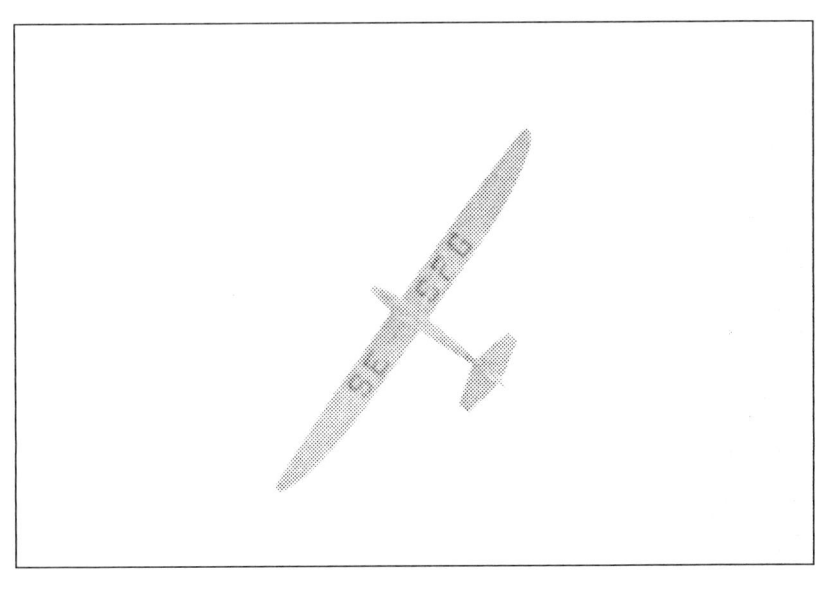

A "real" glider soaring way up in the sky.

"stick" to lift the trainer slightly off the ground, about three feet or so, make a short flight, and land on the grass.

This first exercise was a little frightening to me since at first I could not get off the ground, then rose much too high, way above the treetops. Concentrating on everything that I had learned about gliders and soaring, I somehow managed to complete the flight and made a good landing on the grassy field. After that it became easier and I felt that I was in better control. And after three "solos" with the tow rope disengaged, I had completed the requirements for the first soaring diploma, which was very rewarding to me and also made my husband very happy. Since by that time I was pregnant with my first child, we agreed that this was enough for me.

My pregnancy progressed very normally with no problems, not even morning sickness, so I kept working until about a month before the baby was due, expecting a perfectly normal birth. However shortly thereafter I awoke one morning with a terrible headache, which was quite unusual for me. I decided to go and see my doctor about it later that day. But before I could start getting breakfast ready, I suddenly fainted. I have no recollection of what happened next nor of the following three days. My husband took me to the hospital and the doctors decided to operate the same afternoon and deliver the baby by C-section.

When I regained consciousness four days later, my husband was at my bedside. I was surprised about finding myself in a hospital and he explained that I had become very ill and that we now had a baby boy. He did not mention the operation and I was still somewhat puzzled that all this could happen without my knowing more about it. The baby was about a month premature and weighed about five pounds, but he was healthy and soon doing fine, so I did not worry too much about it.

Only later did I get the whole story. But the cause of the sudden illness—toxemia-eclampsia syndrome—was not clear at the time.

Soon I was home again with the baby, who grew nicely, ate well, and slept well. We called him Rein. He got a lot of attention from his grandmother and from friends and relatives, which he soon learned to accept with a lot of charm.

After a couple of months I returned to my job while my mother took care of the baby during the day. I walked home for lunch, which gave me a little more time with them.

We followed the political events in Europe and were very disappointed that the end of World War Ii did not restore the freedom to our homeland and to the other eastern European countries that had been occupied by the Soviet Union. There did not seem to be any hope for a return to a free Estonia and we had no inkling how anything like that could even become possible.

So we made the best of our life in Sweden while still not abandoning hope that things might change some day. Our Estonian citizenship was recognized only by Britain and the United States, both of which had never officially recognized the occupation of the Baltic States by the Soviet Union. We were not Swedish citizens either, since that required seven years of living in Sweden. To ease the situation, the Swedish government gave us "Swedish Foreigner's Passports" for identification purposes. These were accepted by many countries and allowed us to make a trip to Holland to visit my good friend Nina and her husband.

We had managed to get in touch with each other again. Nina, who had lost her home during the bombing of Tallinn, had left Estonia a few weeks before us with a ship that went to Germany. There she met a young Dutch fellow who had been taken to Germany to work for the Nazis. When the war was over, they got married and my friend could accompany him to Holland. It was great to see her again and to meet her husband and we became good friends. There was so much to talk about. They lived in Nijmegen, which had seen important battles during the war, and we made a bicycle trip to Arnhem, where large numbers of gliders and allied paratroopers had landed during the invasion and visited the huge cemeteries with endless rows of white crosses.

Meanwhile, my sister and her two-year-old son had left for the United States. She had been born in Vladivostok and got her visa under the Russian quota and her son, born in Sweden, could use the Swedish quota. Her husband followed them two years later. My cousin Ellen and her family, including her husband, who had also made it to Sweden, immigrated to Canada, which had different rules and regulations. Several of my friends and former colleagues also left for Canada, hoping to start their own enterprises.

Communications with our homeland were still very difficult. We knew from our own experience how dangerous it was for those living in a communist country to receive letters from abroad. You were instantly suspected of being a spy. My husband still had not been able to contact his parents or even to tell them that he was alive. Then my mother found the address of an Estonian woman she knew who had married a Czech and was living in Prague. She wrote a short greeting to her and included a wedding picture of Helmut and me, asking her to send it, if possible, to an address in Estonia, Helmut's parents, without any further explanation. Since Czechoslovakia was also a communist country behind the Iron Curtain, we felt that communication between that country and Estonia would be far less suspicious or interesting for censors than any letter from Sweden. Weeks went by without any word. Then my mother received a letter from her friend and in it was a short message written by Helmut's father:

"Thank you, dear relative, for remembering us. We were very glad to hear from you. And thanks for sending a picture of your granddaughter's wedding. We like the bride very much. Let us know how things are with you. Wishing you good health and the best to all of you."

The letter had reached its destination and we were greatly relieved. Of course Helmut's parents, for quite a while, were thinking that we were living in Czechoslovakia, but at least they knew that he was alive and that we were married. Years later it became possible to inform his parents, also in an indirect way, that we were in fact living in Sweden and that they had a grandson.

In 1952 my mother received a letter from the U.S. Embassy that her immigration visa could soon be made available, but that she just needed some additional documents, including her husband's death certificate. This seemed like another big problem since my father had died eighteen years earlier at sea and my mother did not have any documentation of it. But I wrote a letter to the harbor captain in Lisbon, Portugal, where the ship had returned after my father's death and surprisingly, we received an answer from Lisbon with the necessary transcript.

I accompanied my mother to the U.S. Embassy and she urged me to ask about my own visa status. After I got married, my husband had also sent in an application for an immigration visa, but so far nothing had been said about us. The person we were talking to checked the records and announced that when I got married, I lost my number on the waiting list. That was news to me! I didn't know what to say, but it did not worry me too much. My mother, however, was very disappointed and started questioning whether she should accept the visa and leave or stay in Sweden. I tried to reassure her as much as I could and when the day of departure came, I took the train ride with her to Gothenburg, the port on the west coast of Sweden from where the ocean liners left for America. Soon she was on board the *MS Drottningholm* and on her way to the New World.

Back in Södertälje my life was changing, too. I told my boss that I would not be able to work any more because I had to take care of my son. The manager, Mr. Ericson, did not want to hear that! He came up with several ideas of his own to solve the problem. The most unexpected of these was to take my son to a park in the morning and to pick him up after work. I told him that I did not think that this would work at all. Then he made an arrangement with a Swedish family who had a son of about the same age as my son, that Rein could stay with them during the day so they could play together and Rein could learn some Swedish. I thought that we could give it a try.

For a few months it worked quite well, but when the Swedish family later left for their summer home on an island, I had to resign for good. I had worked for the company for almost eight years and I had really enjoyed it. When we needed more workers and my boss asked if I knew of some friends who needed a job, I had even gotten jobs for two of my former Estonian colleagues. We all got along very well. However those friends later got married and had left for Canada. Still, I had mixed feelings about leaving, but I knew that it was necessary. However, I kept in touch with my Swedish colleagues and we remained good friends. In Sweden, just like in Estonia, it takes time to become good friends. It does not happen overnight and you really get to know the person first. But once you do become friends, you remain friends for life.

Life in the "Old Kingdom" was very pleasant. We had many friends, both Swedish and Estonian; people would drop by for a cup of coffee, and there were "international" dinner parties with great food and great conversations or discussions on a variety of subjects. There were movies to go to and, since Stockholm was not far away, the Royal Opera, where we saw and heard Jussi Björling sing the title role in *Il Trovatore*, which was a wonderful experience. Another memorable one was T.S. Elliot's play *The Cocktail Party*, which was so highly recommended that we just had to go to the Royal Dramaten, the famous theater, where many Swedish celebrities have started their careers. The play left a strong and lasting impression on us and the cast, with Anita Björk in the leading role, was magnificent.

I also enrolled in a French conversation course given by the Stockholm University and the French Institute. We covered a lot of newer French literature of the twentieth century, including Sartre,

Klosterman, and my special favorite, Antoine de St. Exupéry. There were also short films, poetry and a lot of very interesting discussions with the other participants, all Swedes, except for the French teacher and me. We met in private homes and it was very enjoyable.

A lot of weekends were, of course, spent at the little glider airport, flying and picnicking and just enjoying the Nordic summers. By this time I had a second son, Priit, and a little daughter, Vaike, and they gladly came along wherever we went.

My mother was a little worried about the fact that we were so far away and both she and my sister kept writing and asking me to "do something" about the immigration visas. I did not see what I could do about that. Bureaucracy has its own rules! Then one day I received another questionnaire from the U.S. Embassy asking whether we were still interested in immigrating to the USA. I decided to go there myself and this time I asked to talk to "the person in charge." That person happened to be a woman, somewhat older than myself, good-looking, and obviously very efficient. We talked about my situation and I said the following:

"What is the point of sending me these questionnaires, if nobody can give me any real answers about when we could get an immigration visa? Nearly twelve years ago when I first applied for a visa, I was single, but now I am married and have three children. I was told that I lost my number on the waiting list because I got married and I don't see why any country should punish me for that. My mother, my sister and her family, my aunt, and my uncle live in the United States with their families and have provided the necessary affidavits, etc. If you are not planning to give us a visa, then you can just take us off your list and we shall stay in Sweden."

The lady looked at me in amazement and said, "Who told you such things? This is not true. I shall send a telegram to Washington today and you shall have an answer very soon."

Thank you, Madam Ambassador! Looking back at it now, I am quite sure that's who it was, although it was not mentioned at the time. For who else could have made that kind of a statement!

A day or two later we did get the answer. Visas would be issued to me and my family immediately, but we would have to accept them within the next twenty-four hours or lose them. The visas would be valid for three months.

This was all very unexpected. My husband, who was then working as an electrical engineer in a company that he liked, was not even sure that he really wanted to drop everything and start all over in another country on a different continent. It was no longer an easy decision, now that we had become more settled in Sweden.

"Look what you've done now!" was his comment.

And I did not know what to answer. After some very intense discussions, we decided to give it a try and to accept the visas. I called the Swedish-American line and booked passage on one of their ocean liners for the month of August after finding out that the earlier trips were already sold out. This gave us several months to take care of all the other details. However, when I wrote to my relatives about our plans, they urged us not to leave things to the last minute and to check with the shipping company about possible cancellations. And so our departure was changed to the *MS Stockholm* in the month of July.

There was still a lot to do, to decide what to take with us and what to do with the rest of our furniture and belongings. We ended up giving away a lot of things to our friends who came to say goodbye and our superintendent promised to take care of the rest.

We took the overnight train to Gothenburg, arriving there early in the morning, and spent some time looking for one suitcase, which had somehow become separated from the rest, then boarded the beautiful white ocean liner. Our cabin was lovely, with big windows and lots of space—probably an upgrade due to a cancellation.

A former Swedish colleague and her husband who happened to be vacationing on the west coast of Sweden came to say farewell and to see us off. There was a departure ceremony, with both the Swedish and the American national anthems played by a band. Although we shared a feeling of sadness about leaving Sweden, where we had begun to feel very much at home, we had a sense of adventure about the future in America. There were, of course, also questions in our mind about whether this was the right decision for the family, and I could not help wondering about how it would affect us all. But we did promise our friends that if things went well, we would be returning to Sweden for a visit.

We did not talk much about it, but many of these thoughts crossed my mind as we watched the anchors being raised and the coast line of Sweden disappearing from sight.

We were on our way to the New World. There was a sense of excitement in the air, a beautiful ocean liner to explore, all kinds of shipboard activities, an indoor swimming pool to try out, and time to relax on comfortable deck chairs.

A Captain's Daughter

The weather was good with bright sunshine, except for one day in the middle of our trip when we encountered, what had been called by my father, an "old wave." The sun was still shining and there were just some nice cumulus clouds overhead, but the ship started rolling considerably, although it had a built-in stabilizer which was supposed to keep such things to a minimum.

That day a lot of passengers became acquainted with seasickness and I was the only one in our family who went to the dining room for breakfast, while the others preferred to stay in bed. The dining room was almost empty, so many other passengers must have felt the same way.

In the afternoon of that same day, there was a party scheduled for the children. Luckily, by then my younger son, who was three years old, had managed to get his "sea legs" and decided to go to the party. I took him there and he told us later that he had a great time.

One nice sunny day the passengers were invited to visit the bridge. My husband and I used the opportunity to look around and admire the state-of-the-art navigational equipment, including the radar, which would ensure better safety to passengers and crew. The *MS Stockholm* was certainly very modern and very impressive, a beautiful ocean liner built for travel and pleasure. Little did we know—and who could have imagined it—that this would be the last trip for the *MS Stockholm*, at least under that name!

Chapter 8
Starting All Over in the U.S.A.

We arrived to the New York area on July 22, 1956. A thick fog covered the whole region. The visibility was zero. We heard fog horns and ship sirens all around us, but could not see anything at all. This gave it all a kind of eerie feeling, for we were obviously in a very highly trafficked place. We were told by the ship's captain that it would not be safe to enter into the New York harbor under these conditions and that the ship would be anchored just outside of it until the weather improved.

The following morning was sunny and bright. The fog had disappeared and our ship continued its journey, passing the magnificent Statue of Liberty and moving on to the Hudson River pier.

My sister and brother-in-law were waiting for us on the pier and when the greetings and the arrival formalities were over, they drove us to their new home in a suburb north of the city. My mother was there waiting for us and happy to see the grandchildren. We were all happy to see her too and there was much to talk about.

My sister and her husband both worked in the city and Helmut got a job with the same engineering company where my brother-in-law worked. I stayed at home, helping my mother with housework and shopping, taking care of the kids, and arranging a story hour for them, which they all enjoyed.

We had decided to teach our children Estonian first, so that they could communicate with our relatives and friends, no matter which country they happened to live in and also because we knew that it would be difficult to learn it later, since Estonian is very different from most other languages. From my own experience I knew that children can pick up the local language very easily. My older son had attended school in Sweden for two years and had learned to speak

Swedish well enough. During our transatlantic trip I had taught him a little English and he learned more playing with other children in the area. And so when school started, he entered the third grade and had no big problems, adjusting quickly to the new system and the new friends.

Meanwhile, two days after our arrival, the *MS Stockholm* started its return journey to Sweden. A thick fog was again blanketing the area and not very far from New York, the ship collided with the Italian ocean liner the *Andrea Doria*, which sank within a few hours. Most of its passengers were picked up by *MS Stockholm* and several other ships that had hurried to the accident scene, but about fifty people died in the catastrophe. The *MS Stockholm*, with its bow badly damaged, made it back to New York on its own. It was later repaired and sold to another company and could still be sailing the seven seas under a different name.

How could this have happened with all the modern navigation equipment, that was available, that we had seen with our own eyes while it was demonstrated by the ship's officers?

I tried to follow the investigations and the eventual Maritime Court case. It seemed that both ships were aware of each other and had seen each other on their radar, although they had no visual contact because of the fog. In such situations, according to the international maritime laws, both vessels have to make a right turn to avoid a collision. And that was what the Swedish ship did. The captain of the *Andrea Doria*, however, felt that this would take too much time and make its arrival to New York several hours late. He further assumed that the blip on the radar—the other ship—was probably a much smaller and slower vessel and that he could easily get past in front of it without changing the course of the *Andrea Doria*. What a sad mistake! In spite of all the technological improvements, the human error can still sometimes be the decisive factor.

We soon bought a car, the "Beetle," and I learned to drive. I was told that this was an absolute necessity in America. My husband was my teacher and he drove me to my first driving test in New York City because he could then go on to his job and I could take the train back home. Unfortunately I did not pass the test because of a left turn, which was not "correctly approached." But we tried again and I did get my license eventually. It would, of course, have been much easier for me to take the test in the suburbs, where the traffic was much lighter, but I was not given the choice. It was good to be able to drive locally, to go to the stores and to take the kids to the movies or other activities. We all got along nicely, went to outings together in state parks, to the pools and beaches, and also to the city.

When my sister and brother-in-law suggested that we four could drive to Toronto during the Labor Day weekend, since we all had friends there we, of course, agreed gladly. We left on a Friday afternoon and made a stop in Niagara Falls to admire the beautiful scenery. We then drove all night and arrived in Toronto, Canada, on Saturday. We stayed at our cousin Ellen's house, went our separate ways at times to visit our different friends and then, with help from our friends, got together again at the home of other friends we all knew. It was a whirlwind of a trip, but somehow typical of the New World.

As soon as we felt that we could afford it, we started looking around for a house of our own. We found a small Cape Cod-style house that we liked, in the same village, within walking distance of my relatives' home, and bought it, using all our savings and borrowing some more from very helpful friends. We were already familiar with the area and my son could continue to go to the same school. Soon my younger son and two years later, my daughter, started in kindergarten, and we all made new friends. For a while I even became involved with the PTA, although I never felt that I was the right type of person for that.

As the years went by, we continued to spend many summer vacations in Canada, at Lake Simcoe north of Toronto, where Hilja, a former colleague of mine from the shipping department, and her husband had a summer cottage. We were very good friends and had a standing invitation. The boys spent some time at a camp organized by Canadian-Estonians, which was very good for the kids and relatively inexpensive.

My husband was still working in downtown New York for the same company for the seventh year when it became evident to him that the firm was not doing very well. People were being laid off and he felt that things were coming apart. He had not been very happy with the job, feeling that he did not have the same responsibilities and opportunities that he had had in Sweden and, at times, I wondered about whether the move to the United States had been good for his career. We had talked about other possibilities, but he was not sure what to do about it. Now, however, he felt that it was time to take some days off from work and to start visiting employment offices. I kept typing resumés. Within a week he had another job in the engineering department of a large corporation, with headquarters in midtown Manhattan, just a few minutes from Grand Central train station. The company had plants in many states and soon Helmut was involved in projects in several of these plants and also with the start-up of new plants in a southern state and later in Brazil. He obviously enjoyed his new job and felt appreciated by the company.

We became citizens of the United States. With all the children in school, I started thinking about going back to work to help pay for our new Mustang and for the vinyl siding on our house, needed in order to simplify the maintenance of it. But I wasn't sure where to start. My relatives had told us that any previous job in some other country was totally irrelevant, only the American experience counted now. This, however, did not seem true. Helmut, with his knowledge and widespread experience in electronics and electrical engineering, was doing very well. I myself had managed to do well enough in my earlier jobs and had even done a little part-time work locally for a supplier of textbooks for schools in our area. But mostly I had been a homemaker for more than ten years. I had helped to renovate our home; done some decorating and wallpapering; worked in the garden planting snowdrops, crocuses, and tulips that my friend Nina had sent from Holland; taken long walks with my friend Sigrid, whom I had met at the schoolbus stop when our children started in kindergarten and who was very well informed about local plants and wildflowers and provided me with many more things to plant. I had also learned to play bridge and spent many afternoons with newly found friends doing just that and drinking cups of coffee while discussing local and international problems. It was all very pleasant, but I was still not sure how to approach the job issue.

Then one day a letter arrived by mail. It was from an agency for temporary office workers, pointing out new opportunities. I called them up, went for an interview and was given some tests involving typing and accounting type of work, and soon after that was offered a temporary job of one week at a company located further north from us, involving inventories.

Again a wire company—just like my very first job in Estonia! I also had to pick up another worker hired for the same job who did not have a car. Although there was more driving involved than I had originally planned, I accepted the job, not wanting to refuse the very first job offered. When we arrived at the work site, we found that there were three more "temps" coming to work on the same project. I suppose that we were good workers, for we finished the job in only four days and I got my first paycheck in the United States. On the way home on our last day, while talking with my companion worker, we took a wrong turn somewhere and managed to get lost in a private estate, thereby adding another twist to that particular experience.

The next job was for a bigger company, but luckily in our own community, and involved some type of regional restructuring. That job also lasted a week. I started to like the role of a temporary worker. There was variety, I got to see what American companies were like and how the system worked, and I could take time out when necessary for one reason or another. I also had the choice of accepting a job or refusing it. I quickly became a lot more confident about working in the United States.

My third job was with a large corporation about twenty minutes from my home by car. I had heard from the other "temps" that this was a great place for working and looked forward to a new experience.

This was the headquarters of General Foods, at the time the biggest food company in the country. The building was huge and had nice offices and working areas, a large cafeteria, and plenty of parking space.

I started working on a new project that had never been done before. My boss told me that it had to do with the honesty of the American people and to see whether there were differences in that aspect between the various regions of the country, in order to decide which marketing strategies would be best for each region.

Since the country is very big and the products of the company were sold in every town and village in every single state, there was a lot of data that had to be prepared so that eventually computers—and only big ones existed at the time—could give some kind of answer to the big question.

The job was huge and I became acquainted not only with the big cities, but also with places with names like Rosebud and White Bear Lake and supermarkets with even stranger names. With all the data that had to be processed and coded, we soon had up to ten temporaries working on it, most of them for shorter periods, and since I was by that time quite familiar with the job, I became the "temporary supervisor." There was a lot to learn and I enjoyed the experience and liked the people.

The job went on and on and my boss said jokingly that he would keep me working as long as I wanted to work. He even mentioned that if I wanted a permanent job, he would give me a recommendation for it, but said that in such a case the personnel department would decide where to place me. I preferred, for the time being, to continue in the same manner, since it did give me more flexibility and I could take time off when needed during the holiday season, when schools were closed. But since I took my job seriously, I ended up practically working most of the time. However, when my boss left the company for another job, I decided that maybe this was the time to become a permanent employee. I was not sure how things would work out with a new supervisor who knew less about that particular job than I did. When I sort of mentioned the subject, it was quickly arranged to make the job permanent. I filled out some forms for the personnel department and was interviewed by the director of the corporate marketing research department.

"Why do you want to work?" he asked me.

"Well, I have worked before and I always intended to get back to working some day. Besides, I have a son who is starting in college soon and another one in high school, and therefore some additional income could be useful."

He agreed with that. Then he asked me about the foreign languages on my application form.

"Do you read or write or speak them?"

"All three," was my answer.

He did not find anything else to say, except that he would see what could be done. And so I became a regular employee, with a slightly higher salary than I had before, but also with many benefits, a two-week paid vacation, and health insurance among them.

The job, meanwhile, continued for a few months and then came the final result, a computer print-out which showed that there were real differences in the various regions of the country. I was told that this was the first time that a computer program had been used in the company to make marketing decisions. Everybody seemed to be rather exited about that and I was glad to have been part of it all.

Our department was growing and soon some of us were moved to a different area in the huge building, and several months later, there was a restructuring in the company and we moved again to a yet another part of the building. At that time new subgroups were formed and I was told that I would have a new job and a new boss. That was understandable, since after the original job was finished I had been working on several other projects. But I had also found out through the "grapevine" that a change had been made in my job classification that I did not know about. So when I had an interview with my new supervisor, a young lady who had just joined our department, I used the opportunity to ask her about the title and the salary of my new job, saying that there had been some irregularities earlier that I wanted to avoid.

My new supervisor seemed a little startled about my question and after a pause, she said that she did not know about that and would get back to me later. I felt that something strange was going on and started thinking about looking around for another job myself. Having at that point a lot more experience about the American job market, I was convinced that I could find another job without much difficulty. Although I liked the company, I felt instinctively that I was not being treated fairly and yet I could not put my finger on the problem. Therefore, during a lunch hour, I went to an employment agency to see what was available.

The person who was interviewing me was certain that she could get me another job, but asked why I wanted to leave my present company, since it was known as a good corporation to work for.

I gave a short explanation without wanting to go into details. Then my interviewer suggested that before quitting my job, I should go and talk to someone in the personnel department about the situation. I felt that I had nothing to lose and made an appointment with the person who had been mentioned as very good and capable.

I was, of course, again asked questions and had to explain why I felt so uncertain and uncomfortable about my job situation.

"So you are starting a new job within the company and you don't know what the job title is or what the salary is?" she asked me. "I am going to look into this and let you know."

I was afraid that I was making more waves than I had intended, but it was too late to back down now. A few days later, the manager of the group to which I had been assigned told me that I had an appointment to see someone in the personnel department.

"Do you know who he is?" he asked.

"No, I don't, but I shall find out," was my answer.

I did find out quickly that the person was the director of corporate personnel. We met at the appointed hour and after a few questions, Mr. D.C.P. said, "But you were only a temporary."

"I do not consider it a disgrace to work for a company like General Foods on a temporary basis. After being away from the job market for years because of family obligations, working as a temporary gave me a chance to see what the job market was like and what kind of jobs could be available to me. But I have had other jobs before and my supervisors have always been very satisfied with my work. I have also been on the board of directors of a shipping company and I did a good job there, too. And when I was offered a permanent job as an analyst by this company I was glad to accept it."

I just had to mention the shipping company because of Mr. D.C.P.'s slightly overbearing tone. That episode had actually happened during my last years in Sweden when the remaining assets of our former shipping company had been acquired by a Swedish-Estonian firm and an annual meeting was called in Stockholm to deal with the situation. My relatives in United States and Canada had sent me the powers to represent their interests and together with my cousin Thelma, who represented her own family, we managed to avoid a total loss. After that, to my surprise, I became a member of the board of directors of the new firm and finally a better than expected solution was found to the problems. Of course, I had never mentioned that on my job application.

Mr. D.C.P. listened, but made no comment. Then he said, "But the classification was Analyst T.B.E." (meaning To Be Evaluated).

"There was no T.B.E. on my paper," I answered.

"What paper?"

"The one that I received from the personnel department, the white copy. The blue and yellow copies went to others in the company."

"But didn't you think that the salary was rather small for the classification?"

"Maybe I did. But I had no way of knowing what the salary categories were in the company. And it was more than I had been getting before."

I was so glad that I had kept that white copy in my files! There was some more talk about the job and the company, ending with some vague statements. But I still did not know, what the solution would be. I kept on working in the new group and found the job very uninteresting compared to what I had been doing before.

I had, by that time, been employed on a permanent basis for more than a year and earned my vacation. Helmut and I had planned a great vacation in Europe, spending some time in Sweden as we had promised to our friends, and making some other stops besides. We were looking forward to it and felt that we really deserved it. It was thirteen years after we had left Sweden.

Now suddenly it was uncertain whether there would be a job for me on our return. It was a very uneasy situation. The new supervisor who had interviewed me after the restructuring was nowhere to be seen. I felt that things were going on behind the scenes, but there was nothing more that I could do except to wait and see what happened.

One afternoon as I was driving home from work through my usual backroads in order to avoid traffic jams, my car was lightly bumped by a big blue van driving behind me. This had never happened to me on the road and without even thinking, I just kept on driving. The van was following me, taking every turn that I took. Was this a coincidence? It was like something from a Hollywood movie. I got very nervous and my knees were shaking.

I knew that I had been "rocking the boat" more than I ever intended or imagined. Some people might be very angry at me, thinking that this whole incident might affect their careers too, since decent companies do not like "dirty tricks." As soon as I could, I took a turn to the main road and pulled into the parking lot of a big shopping center. The van kept going and disappeared. And I made it home with a big sigh of relief.

A week or two went by, our vacation was coming closer, and I had still not heard anything more about the situation. Then one morning, a manager in our department who was in charge of marketing trends asked me to step by in his office. I did not know him very well, but some time ago when I was still a "temp," I had been asked to do some work for him with trend charts when the person who worked for him was hospitalized. I wasn't very happy about being pulled away from my own job, but he had been very nice, explaining everything thoroughly, and so I got the job done and even discovered some mistakes that had to be corrected. The analytical geometry that I had learned in high school and had considered totally unnecessary at the time became very useful after all.

Without saying a word about the existing controversy, the manager smiled and asked, "Would you like to work for me as a statistical analyst? I know that you can do the job for you have already done it before." He then mentioned the salary, definitely a promotion.

This was totally unexpected, like a so-called "white knight" out of the blue. And he was certainly a very nice person, so I did not have to think much—this would solve my problem. But was he aware of what was going on? I started hesitatingly, "Well, if everybody is willing to...." I stopped, looking for the right word.

"To bury the hatchet?" he said with a smile.

We both started to laugh and of course I agreed with the proposal.

"But I have a vacation scheduled. What about that?" I asked.

"That's fine. And when you come back, you will be working for me." He also mentioned that the other person who had been working for him would be moving to another job in the company.

Suddenly things were back on track. What a wonderful feeling that was! And we could leave for our vacation, happy and care-free.

At the time, it was possible to plan your vacation so that you paid the fare to the most distant point on your trip and you were allowed to make as many stops on the way as you wanted, as long as you flew in the same direction. This worked out very well for us.

Our first stop was in Paris, the beautiful city that I had heard and read so much about. Just to be there, to walk around, and to admire all the famous sights and places so full of history was wonderful. And although we had no reservations, we managed to get a table at the restaurant on top of the Eiffel tower, had a very good dinner, and were given two framed menus as a souvenir. Together with some American tourists, we then watched the lights go on all over Paris. It was not a foreign country to me; I felt perfectly at home and left with the feeling that I must come back there soon.

We then visited my friend Nina and her husband Jan in Holland and together with our friends, we watched Neil Armstrong land on the moon. Then after a stop in Copenhagen and another in Lund, in the southern tip of Sweden to pay a visit to cousin Thelma, her husband Max, and her mother, we flew on to Stockholm to meet with friends living in that area. I also called my former Swedish colleagues and we agreed to meet at the Canal Café, situated on a small hill near the Canal of Södertälje, which unites the Lake of Mälaren with the Baltic Sea. As we were approaching the café, I saw Ines and Ingrid coming down the long row of stairs to meet us and after a warm greeting, one of them said softly, "Look who else is here!"

I looked up, and to my great surprise saw my former boss, Mr. Ericson, and his wife standing on top of the hill. One of my friends had crossed paths with Mr. Ericson in a store and had mentioned about our planned get-together. He had then asked if he could join us and brought his wife along, too.

We sat down on the patio and chatted about old times and exchanged news about our lives, both in Sweden and the New World, while enjoying the scenery and the beautiful Nordic summer. The boss even picked up the tab, which amused my Swedish friends very much.

It was really very nice and we were touched by the fact that after thirteen years he would take the trouble and the time to join us all.

The Östra Sörmlands Flying Club had arranged a big reunion at the airport where we used to spend so many weekends. Many of the old-timers were there with their families. There was a lot of flying and soaring and Helmut was honored with a flag of the club and a book about its history. In the late afternoon we all drove across a bridge to a small island where one of the members had a summer cottage and where the celebration continued for hours. What a welcome that was, more than we had ever expected!

On the way home, we made a short stop in London to refresh old memories, and then it was time to return home again.

My new job was quite interesting and covered the market trends for all our products. Soon it was decided to acquire marketing information regularly from other countries in Europe, South and Central America, Canada, Mexico, Japan, and Australia, where the company had subsidiaries, and I started working on worldwide trends. My boss told me that this had never been done before and that it was now possible because of "my languages." It was, of course, a lot of work, but I was ready for the challenge. When I got together the new worldwide reports and the trend charts, the head of the Corporate Marketing Research Department made presentations on a bi-monthly basis to the top management. Everybody was anxious to get on the list for my worldwide reports, but I was told to limit these to about thirty executives and not to include any others without special permission from the boss.

Every few years there were restructurings in the company. People retired, among them my boss, or they were transferred to other departments or promoted to new positions. I was often reporting to new supervisors who knew very little about my work. Some people in our department told me that I was a fool to do all this work because I was not being paid for it. But I had gotten pay raises regularly, I liked the job, and enjoyed the camaraderie and the variety of people I got to know in the corporate world, as well as the office parties, the Christmas lunches, and the big meetings, held usually in some country club.

There was even a French table to which I had been introduced quite early in my career. It included people from different departments and divisions with different positions, some of them native Frenchmen and others of different backgrounds but able to speak the language. We met once a week in the cafeteria for lunch and had great conversations during our lunch hour. I enjoyed it very much.

One day many of us received a letter from the personnel department suggesting that we should take control of our own careers and that the company was willing to help us by providing various workshops and even college courses, realizing that many people, women in particular, had to interrupt their education for personal reasons.

I decided to sign up for the program. During the first year the professors came to the company location and we got our instruction in a somewhat informal setting, right after work. It was very interesting. After the first two semesters, we were on our own. To continue, we had to have our previous education evaluated and to matriculate in the nearby Pace University.

There was no stopping now. It took a lot of effort to put all the documentation together, to make the translations and copies, and to drive to the university during my lunch hour to meet with professors, who wanted to check out all the information, but it was certainly worthwhile.

I got credit for many courses that I had taken in Europe and also for the languages, even for some of the work that I was already doing in marketing and for which samples were provided.

I continued taking business-related courses for the next three years. Although at first I had been primarily interested in completing the requirements for a college degree, certainly useful in a big corporation, I found that I really enjoyed it and that every course had some extra bonus for me that I had not expected. Studying had always been easy for me and the company paid for the tuition, even for the textbooks. The professors were excellent and the students represented a wide variety of people of different age groups. In some courses there was a surprisingly large number of college kids.

I remember particularly the last exam of my very last course. It was expected to be very tough, so the professor told us that he would give us two separate exams and count the better grade of the two for the final grade. Knowing that this was the final one was somehow quite exiting. So far I had done very well and I looked forward to finishing the job. No more term papers and long working days, leaving the house shortly after 8:00 A.M. and returning after 9:00 P.M. twice a week. I felt that I had to take this exam very seriously, and so I took a couple of pencils and pens with me and two calculators, just in case that one would somehow stop working. I wanted to be ready.

When we were all gathered in the classroom, the professor announced the grades for the first exam that we had taken a week earlier. I was very glad to hear that I had gotten a five for it, which meant that I would not have to worry any more. Then, as I settled down to work, I heard a male voice from behind me saying to the professor, "Are you really going to make her take the second test?"

There was a pause, then, turning to me, the professor said, "Actually, you don't have to take this test. You can go home."

I was stunned at the unexpected turn of events, thanked the professor, picked up my belongings, and walked out of the room. It was over! I had no idea who the guy was who posed the question, but I was very grateful and I hope that he realized it.

After the graduation ceremony, I invited my mother and the rest of my family for lunch at a nearby restaurant where buffalo meat and game birds were on the menu. I wanted to do something unusual and it sounded very American.

At work there was a little party too, in our marketing library. It was a total surprise for me. A promotion followed and soon, as one of the ten first people who had participated in the program and gotten a degree and a promotion, I was invited to a lunch in the executive dining room, which was hosted by a vice president who was in charge of the program. All in all it was a great experience.

During the following years, there were more responsibilities, more promotions, and more restructurings in the company, and I became part of the International Marketing Research group.

Computers in the 1970s had made my life a little easier, when after a two-day course I had learned how to access a large computer in New York City by telephone, which enabled me to load in all the previous as well as the current marketing data and have the computer do the work, providing a print-out. This worked well for a while, but in spite of code words and other measures that were taken, at times I ran into unexpected complications and our programs did not work properly. So as soon as Apple came out with a personal computer, I was given one for my own work and that made things much better.

I enjoyed working in the international group, even the chance of going on a business trip. We had great discussions, among other things, about the metric system. I was always for it, since I had grown up with it and knew the advantages of it. All the data from the rest of the world came in metrics and had to be recalculated into pounds and gallons, etc. Even the United Kingdom had at that time made the decision to switch to the metric system, something that was deeply regretted by the British member of our group, who found the old-

The graduation

fashioned system far more romantic. Well, we in this country have not yet made the switch and are not even talking about it any more. But I believe that some day in the future it will happen.

Eventually there was another restructuring in the company and a chance for early retirement with relatively good conditions.

There were also take-over rumors. I could hardly take these seriously and I really liked my job, but the prospect of having more time for myself and my family began to look quite attractive.

So after working for three years in Estonia, eight years in Sweden, and sixteen years in the United States, I decided to end my career of an international marketing research analyst and to retire. There was a lovely retirement party for me with beautiful gifts and lots of good wishes. Even bets were made whether the next worldwide report would be out on time, but that was no longer my problem.

With more time for myself, I could catch up with things that I had just pushed aside before. I could spend more time with my mother and find out more about her earlier life. I also got involved with a French conversation group in the neighboring village, which was organized by the French Institute. There were also French cooking classes, new ideas and new recipes, and many very enjoyable afternoons spent with new friends discussing old and new problems.

Since travel is already in my genes, we used every opportunity for traveling and discovery, including a cross-country drive with the Mustang to Grand Canyon and many trips to Canada and Europe, as well as Mexico, South America, the Caribbean islands, Australia, and Tahiti.

Among the most memorable experiences were the sunrises in the Grand Canyon, the French Alps, and Cabo San Lucas in Mexico; climbing the pyramids in Teotihuacan, also in Mexico; admiring the 15,000 year-old cave paintings in Altamira, Spain: the sense of history that I felt on the Acropolis and in the old amphitheaters in Athens and Rome; the majestic Falls of Iguassu; the beaches of the Caribbean and Hawaii; and the dip into the Pacific Ocean, when our dugout canoe rolled over and dumped us into the sea. And meeting with old friends who were now living in many different parts of the world.

What a joy it was and what a beautiful world! There were—and I am sure that there still are—lots of places to discover. No need to worry about that! Especially when traveling as we did, on our own, without strict schedules and mostly without reservations. There were many opportunities to meet local people, to discuss politics in France with the owner of a small restaurant and his son, or lifestyles in

Greece with a schoolteacher, or different cultures in Mexico and Brazil; to admire the vastness of the Central Plains in America and to taste local foods and drinks.

The various airlines, the trains, the ferries, and the rented cars took us to our destinations with few problems and only occasionally with some unexpected adventures, which added their own memories to it all.

There was one place, however, where we could not go—our original homeland, Estonia, which was still occupied by the Soviet Union. Things were slowly changing and it became possible to send letters by mail, but a visit was still risky and complicated by all kinds of formalities.

In 1991 I found out that in connection with a song festival, which was going to take place in Tallinn in the month of July and in which choirs from the USA were participating as well as from many other states of the Soviet Union, it was possible to get a so-called "cultural visa" for $100 per person faxed overnight, and no questions asked. We could not let that opportunity go by and decided immediately to go. It was an unforgettable experience for us.

We flew first to Stockholm and from there to Tallinn. Many of our friends, both mine and my husband's, had come to the airport to meet us. There was also an Estonian choral group to welcome the American singers with a beautiful song which is usually sung at the opening of a song festival. We couldn't help feeling included in the welcome.

After greetings had been exchanged, together with our friends we went to the beautiful home of Kaljo, a friend of my husband, where we spent a lovely evening with lots of talk and food and even some singing.

In spite of the very tense political situation, it was wonderful to be back in Tallinn after nearly forty-seven years, to walk in the "old town," which still looked the same, to meet with old friends, and even to pay a visit to our former home, where now others were living.

We also went to the East/West United Song Festival, Bridges of Song. It had originally been an idea of the American composer John Williams to bring together singers from all the states of the U.S. and all the republics of the USSR and although it did not turn out quite that way, there were choirs from the USA, Canada, Japan, Byelorussia, Moldavia, Latvia, Lithuania, Ukraine, Russia, Georgia, Armenia, Uzbekistan, and some other countries participating. Many of these had separate performances in various concert halls and churches during the first days of the festival. But during the last day, the Grand Finale, all 13,000 singers sang together in English, Estonian, and other languages. It was very moving and many people had tears in their eyes during the last songs, one of which had become a second national anthem after the original national anthem had been banned by the Soviets.

A month after our return, Estonia regained its independence and to our great joy and relief it all happened peacefully, without any fatalities. Thank you, Mr. Williams, for your part in the Singing Revolution!

For my husband it was the only visit to his former homeland. Three years later, we took his ashes back to Estonia and my son Priit had the joy and privilege to participate in another song festival, this time in the free Republic of Estonia, eager to rejoin the free world.

The United States has changed in many ways during the nearly half a century that we have been living here. The question that we sometimes asked ourselves was whether the decision to come here was the right one. I think that for myself and for my husband, it opened up many new opportunities that would not have been possible otherwise. However, it also affected the lives of our children, exposing them to very different cultural influences and situations that we were not able to expect or to prepare them for. I suppose that this is inevitable and has to be dealt with the best you can.

"Can you really feel that you are an American?" That was the question that a pretty young secretary once asked me.

"Why not?" was my answer. "Except for American Indians, everybody in this country has originally come here from somewhere else."

She said that she had not thought about it that way.

But I felt that this was true. In most other countries you would always remain a foreigner, even if you learned to speak the local language and got along well with the people. In the United States things are somewhat different, although here too, there are those who count the generations that their family members have lived here and take this very seriously.

I remember an incident years ago when my older son, who had been attending a college in upstate New York, decided to change his major and transfer to a university in New York City.

A young girl, a good friend of his, who was attending a teacher's college in the same town, decided that she did not want to become a teacher, and at the end of the school year, instead of going home, came here too.

I was completely taken by surprise. She stayed with us at first, but I told her that this was only temporary, that while she had the right to make her own decisions about her life and her career, she should talk it over with her parents. If she really felt strongly about it, then she would have to get an apartment and a job and also continue with her education by taking evening courses. What would her parents say if they found out that she was staying with us? They might think that I had somehow encouraged her in this.

Well, we did not have to wonder about this very long. A few days later, when Rein and Brenda (not her real name) had gone to New York City, the phone rang. It was Brenda's mother.

"Is my daughter Brenda there?" was her question.

"No, she's not."

"But she is staying with you?"

"Yes, she has been staying here at present."

Then the mother said something that upset me and also angered me: "I am going to take legal steps against you."

"What do you want me to do? Throw her out on the street? Believe me, I am not any more interested of all this than you are."

At this point, the mother's tone changed a little and she asked, "Tell me, why does my daughter do this to me?"

"Your daughter is a very quiet person. I don't know why she does this to you or to me."

We ended up talking more peacefully. I promised to do what I could to have Brenda call her and to advise her to discuss her plans for the future with her family.

Little by little I found out that Brenda's mother and grandmother were both teachers and wanted her to continue with the family tradition. Brenda felt that her mother was too overpowering and that she would not be able to stand up to her on this issue. Her family also considered themselves fifth-generation Americans, which added another little twist to it. It made me aware of how status-conscious people can be even in this "land of the free."

Well, after about two weeks, Brenda did get an apartment as well as a job in New York City. She also told me that she was taking college courses in the evening and that she had called her mother and talked to her. But she did not have the courage to go home for Christmas and spent the holidays with us.

At Easter time Brenda was finally ready to face her parents. My son drove her home, together with her two cats and several hamsters.

He felt that it would be unsafe for her to drive for hours "with all those animals." Later I heard that he had to stay in a motel and was never invited to Brenda's home to meet her parents or even for a cup of tea. That did seem rather unfair to me, for I would have expected a little friendlier attitude, even toward a first-generation American.

I feel that after having been a citizen of several countries, including one citizenship that was not by choice but forced upon us by an occupying state, after having traveled in many other countries and continents and enjoyed it immensely, I can regard myself also as a citizen of this wonderful world where we all happen to live. As we all know, it's the only one we have!

I do not believe in the melting pot theory that you have to forget everything that you have known before in order to become an American. According to recent statistics, 40 percent of New Yorkers have been born in another country. They are all first-generation Americans, unless of course they decide to keep their previous citizenship.

I remember also hearing an educator speaking years ago in a local high school who, among other things, said that it's a pity that many parents do not teach their children their own native language. It's theirs for free! Research has also shown that it is good for the brain—the ability is there!

As far as "Friday the thirteenth," I think that I made the right choice in believing the good omens and predictions, even superstitions, and disregarding the rest. I certainly have had my share of good luck many times over or I would not even be here writing this memoir. To borrow an expression from the French writer J. P. Sartre (said about totally different subjects), "It has the importance that you choose to give to it."

My wish for an exciting and colorful life has been fulfilled beyond expectations. I have met many wonderful people in many parts of the world and as far as problems and challenges, we all have to expect something in those areas, too. It reminds me of a childhood game that we played long ago, where one person had to walk blindfolded through a "field of obstacles" which were secretly later removed. Those, who already knew the game and were watching, had a good laugh at the whole thing.

So while life has been compared to a rose garden or a box of chocolates, I prefer to look at life as an obstacle course. Some of those can be avoided, others may have to be jumped or climbed over or handled in some other way. It is not always easy, but each time that you manage to do it, you will be rewarded by a sense of satisfaction and a greater confidence in yourself and your own abilities. You will become a survivor.

And, getting back to Vilsandi, the whole island is now a National Park. The farms are all gone, except one on the eastern tip of the island, where the son of the previous owner is now growing ostriches. The lighthouse is still there and also the weather station, which is now sending daily weather reports to Brussels and Washington.

And the birds still come to the Vaika isles every spring for nesting and for raising their young.

Young seagulls in the Vaika isles.

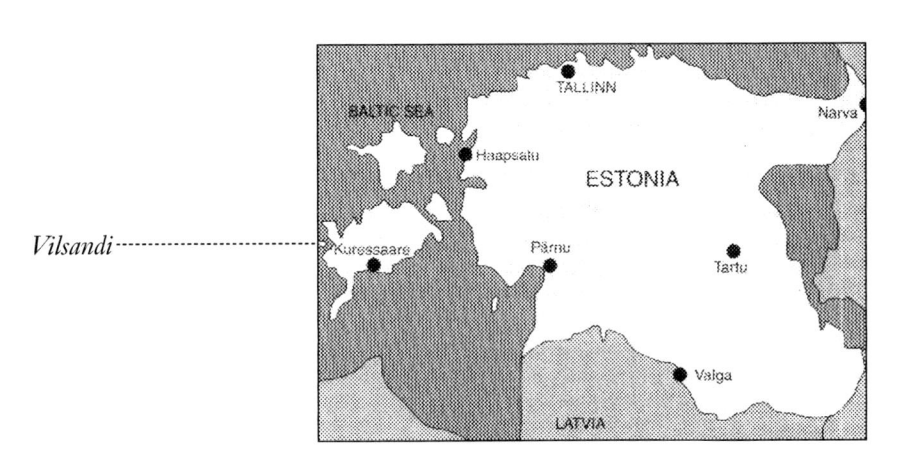

Map of Estonia